# The New Industrial Relations?

## Based on the ED/ESRC/PSI/ACAS Surveys

**Neil Millward**

Policy Studies Institute
London

**PUBLISHING**

**The publishing imprint of the independent
POLICY STUDIES INSTITUTE
100 Park Village East, London NW1 3SR
Telephone: 071-387 2171  Fax: 071-388 0914**

ISBN 0 85374 591 9

PSI Research Report 756

A CIP catalogue record of this book is available from the British Library.

1 2 3 4 5 6 7 8 9

1000159248
• S

PSI publications are available from
BEBC Distribution Ltd
P O Box 1496, Poole, Dorset, BH12 3YD

Books will normally be despatched within 24 hours. Cheques should be made payable
to BEBC Distribution Ltd.

Credit card and telephone/fax orders may be placed on the following freephone
numbers:

FREEPHONE: 0800 262260
FREEFAX: 0800 262266

Booktrade representation (UK & Eire):
Broadcast Books
24 De Montfort Road, London SW16 1LW
Telephone: 081 677 5129

PSI subscriptions are available from PSI's subscription agent
Carfax Publishing Company Ltd
P O Box 25, Abingdon, Oxford OX14 3UE

Laserset by Policy Studies Institute
Printed in Great Britain by BPCC Wheatons Ltd, Exeter

# Contents

*Foreword*
*Acknowledgements*
*Notes on tables used in text*
*List of tables*

## 1 INTRODUCTION   ①

'The new industrial relations'   ②
'Human resource management'   3
The essential features of the WIRS design   4
'Within-unit' change: the 1984-190 panel sample   5
Compositional change   6
    *The sample of panel closures*   7
    *Younger workplaces in the 1990 main sample*   7
    *The 1990 sample of 'new workplaces'*   9
The nature and contents of the book   10


## 2 THE COLLECTIVE REPRESENTATION OF EMPLOYEES   ⑭

Plant closures   15
The characteristics of younger workplaces   19
Union recognition in younger workplaces   21
Employer policy on union recognition   ㉔
Union representation without pay bargaining rights   30


## 3 SINGLE UNION REPRESENTATION   ㉟

Single and multi-union workplaces – union presence   36
    *The industries and unions involved in single-union presence*   39
The nature of single union representation   43
    *Membership density and type of employer*   43
    *Union recognition*   46

*Recent moves towards single union recognition*                50
*Collective bargaining coverage in single-union workplaces*    51
*Union representatives and their facilities*                   51

**4  SINGLE UNION AGREEMENTS, DISPUTES PROCEDURES
    AND MANAGEMENT CONTROL**                                   55

Sole union agreements in workplaces with a single recognised union  55
*Employer characteristics associated with sole union agreements*    56
*Union characteristics associated with sole union agreements*       59
Dispute avoidance and resolution in sole union agreements           62
Union constraints upon management in the organisation of work       66
*Management freedom in single union workplaces*                     69
*Types of single union representation*                              72

**5  EMPLOYEE INVOLVEMENT AND HRM PRACTICES**                  76

The functioning of consultative committees                     81
A broader look at management-employee communication            84
The substance of communication and consultation               95
Employee involvement through financial participation           98
'Single status' employment                                    104

**6  SUMMARY AND CONCLUSIONS**                                117

The retreat of traditional industrial relations              119
Single union representation                                  121
Single union agreements                                      122
*The 'package' of features*                                  125
Human resource management practices                          127
Younger workplaces as a pointer to the future               130

**TECHNICAL APPENDIX**                                        135

The sampling frame and the main 1990 survey sample           135
Questionnaire development and fieldwork                       139
*Pilot work*                                                  139
*Main survey fieldwork*                                       140
Overall response                                              143
Response among worker representatives and financial managers  145
Coding and editing of the data                               147
Weighting of the main sample data                             149

The 1984-1990 trading sector panel sample 150  
The 1990 sample of 'new workplaces' 152  
    *Methodology* 153  
    *Duplicates between A, B, C87 & C90 Groups* 155  
    *Duplicates with 1987 Census of Employment* 155  
    *Duplicates with 1987 or earlier Postcode Directories* 156  
    *Personal PO Box Numbers* 156  
    *Outcome of duplicate checks* 156  
    *Contacting addresses for the 'new workplaces' sample* 157  
    *'Wave 2' approaches* 158  
    *Screening and interviews* 158  
    *Financial managers* 159  
    *Worker representatives (manual)* 160  
    *Worker representatives (non-manual)* 160  
Characteristics of the 'new workplaces' supplementary sample 160  
    *Region and industrial activity* 161  
Sampling errors 161  

*Index* 166

# Foreword

Throughout the 1980s the reform of British industrial relations was high on the agenda of politicians, managers, workers and their trade unions. Vigorous debate took place over what could and should be done, about how best to achieve change and, not least, about the nature, extent and consequences of the developments which were already under way. The Workplace Industrial Relations Survey (WIRS) series was designed to contribute to these continuing debates – and to the better understanding of the processes which underlie employment relationships – by making available for the first time large-scale, systematic and dispassionate evidence about a broad range of industrial relations and employment practices across almost every sector of the economy. The reports on the first two surveys, conducted in 1980 and 1984, were widely welcomed as providing the most comprehensive bank of material on such matters yet available for any developed economy. Not only were the findings much discussed by policy-makers and practitioners within and outside government, but the data were subjected to secondary analysis by academic and other researchers in a range of disciplines. The success of the surveys encouraged governments and researchers in other countries to mount equivalent inquiries. That the venture proved worthwhile cannot be doubted.

The 1990 survey was, as previously, sponsored jointly by the Employment Department, the Economic and Social Research Council, the Policy Studies Institute (with funds from the Leverhulme Trust) and the Advisory, Conciliation and Arbitration Service. As before, each organisation brought its particular interests and concerns in the exercise to a joint steering committee which oversaw the project. That committee first met in 1988 under the chairmanship of Peter Brannen, then Chief Research Officer at the Employment Department. He had been closely involved with the development, design and management of the series since its original conception in the late 1970s, and in the intervening years he made a major contribution to its success. In 1989 he moved elsewhere in the Department and the chair of the committee was then taken, first by Vince Keddie and later by me. All four sponsors record their warm appreciation of the imagination, skill, and cheerful determination to overcome difficulties which Peter brought to discussions, and which played no small part in developing the spirit of positive co-operation between the sponsors which has characterised their meetings.

The lengthy period needed for the planning and execution of a survey as substantial as WIRS meant that many people took part in the work of the steering committee. For the Employment Department they included Neil Millward, Mark Stevens, David Smart, Mike Lott and Andrew Hardman. For the Policy Studies Institute W W Daniel took the lead. For the ESRC responsibilities were taken primarily by Adrian Alsop with A W J Thomson and, later, by Christine McCulloch and Graham Winfield. The ACAS member was W R Hawes, who was helped for part of the period by Andrew Scott. I am grateful to them all, both for the important substantive contributions they made to the design and conduct of the survey and for their readiness to see each others' points of view in aid of the greater good.

A key aim of the WIRS series has been to provide evidence on the way industrial relations and employment relations change over time. Initially it was envisaged that this would be done by undertaking a series of cross-sectional surveys based on a central core of questions which would be asked of similar respondents on each occasion. That approach remains a key element in the project design. Following successful experimental work in 1984, however, it was decided to include in the 1990 design an additional large-scale panel element which would provide a substantial body of longitudinal data. It was also decided that interviews should be attempted in an additional sample of very new establishments which were not caught by the basic sampling frame. All this meant that the survey design, always challenging, took on a new and burdensome complexity in 1990. The detailed and difficult work necessary to bring such a design to fruition was undertaken for the Steering Committee by a research team which included Neil Millward at PSI (on secondment from the Employment Department), Mark Stevens and David Smart at the Employment Department, W R Hawes at ACAS and Colin Airey, Nigel Tremlett, Rosemary Hamilton and other colleagues at Social and Community Planning Research. SCPR have been involved as fieldwork contractors for the WIRS series from its beginning. They once again made the fullest contribution to the design, fieldwork and data processing stages of the survey.

An important feature of the WIRS series has been the determination of the sponsors to provide full and rapid dissemination of its results through some initial publications and through release of the anonymised data for secondary analysis. There are two initial publications in the case of the 1990 survey. The first gave an overall descriptive analysis of the results; it was written by Neil Millward, Mark Stevens, David Smart and W R Hawes and published in September 1992 under the title *Workplace Industrial Relations in Transition*. The second is this volume, written by Neil Millward, which focuses on the extent and nature of new developments in the field. Whilst the volume forms a key part of PSI's contribution to the 1990 WIRS enterprise, the author writes in a personal capacity; interpretations of the results and views expressed upon them should not be taken as necessarily representing the views of any of the sponsoring organisations, which have endorsed the publication of the volume in the expectation of informing public discussion.

As on previous occasions, these books are intended to provide a first word on the results, rather than a last. To encourage more detailed exploration of the survey material, the anonymised data and accompanying documentation have been made freely available to academic and other researchers since early 1992 through the ESRC's Data Archive at the University of Essex. So far over 50 researchers from nearly 40 universities and research centres in Britain and abroad have acquired them. Numerous working papers and many publications have already been produced.

To assist users of the data three further publications have been endorsed by the WIRS sponsors. The first of these is a full technical report of the 1990 survey, by Colin Airey, Nigel Tremlett and Rosemary Hamilton, and is available from SCPR. The second is a guide to questions in all three surveys, written by Mark Stevens and David Smart and published by the Employment Department. The third is a bibliography of analyses based upon the data from the WIRS series; it was compiled by Neil Millward and published by PSI. Regular updates of this bibliography are to produced by the ESRC Data Archive, which is also now establishing a WIRS User Group. These and other initiatives are designed to promote analysis and use of the data by a wider range of people than before. The sponsors unite in hoping that the unparalleled opportunities for secondary analysis presented by the WIRS series will be taken.

The WIRS venture is undoubtedly expensive, but I strongly believe that it is also highly cost effective. It is a periodic survey series of international significance and I hope it will continue to provide a broad analysis of developments in an area which is forever evolving and changing to meet the requirements and aspirations of both employers and employees.

Zmira Hornstein
Chair, Steering Committee for the Workplace
Industrial Relations Surveys.

# Acknowledgements

PSI has been involved as a partner in the WIRS series since it began. On the first survey the Institute made a major contribution to the design and analysis, principally in the person of Bill Daniel. On the second survey, a section of questioning on the introduction and impact of new technology was the focus of the Institute's involvement. Bill Daniel's report on that feature of the 1984 survey, plus a substantial input to the survey sourcebook, were the visible outcomes of the Institute's contribution then. On the third survey PSI focused on new developments and new practices in the field of employee relations. Once again the Institute's involvement was made possible by generous support from the Leverhulme Trust.

I am grateful to Bill Daniel for entrusting to me the task of making the main contribution from the Institute towards seeing the 1990 survey through from the early stages of design to the publication of this report. For most of the time, I was at PSI on secondment from the Employment Department. During that period I was asked to help with the data analysis and the writing of the sourcebook; I was glad to do so. The current report was completed after I had become an employee of the Institute. Throughout the whole period, until recently when he stepped down as the Institute's Director, Bill Daniel made invaluable contributions to the work. I also received help, advice and comments from Bill Hawes, Andrew Wareing and colleagues at PSI.

The success of the WIRS series depends very much on the co-operation and support of the managers and worker representatives who participate in the surveys. I would like to add my personal voice to those of the sponsors and the rest of the research team in thanking the 4,725 individuals who gave freely of their time to be interviewed as part of the 1990 survey.

Neil Millward

# Notes on tables used in the text

## General conventions adopted in tables
§    Unweighted base too low for percentages (see Note A).
( )  Percentages should be treated with caution (see Note B).
..    Data not available (see Note J).
*    Fewer than 0.5 per cent.
-    Zero.

## Notes on tables
(A)  Unweighted base is fewer than 20 and therefore too low for percentages.

(B)  Unweighted base is 20 or more but fewer than 50; percentages should be treated with caution.

(C)  Column and row percentages do not always add to 100 owing to the rounding of decimal points.

(D)  The proportions in subsidiary categories do not always add to the proportion in a composite category owing to the rounding of decimal points.

(E)  Column and row percentages sometimes add to more than 100 because more than one answer was possible.

(F)  The proportions in subsidiary categories do not always add to the proportion in a composite category because more than one answer was possible.

(G)  The base numbers for the individual categories in a variable do not add to the total base number because the necessary information was not provided in a number of cases.

(H)  The weighted base numbers for the individual categories in a variable may not add to the total weighted base number owing to the rounding of decimal points.

(J)  The data are not available because either the question was not asked, or it was asked of a different respondent, or the question was asked in a sufficiently different form to make strict comparisons difficult.

(K)  The base numbers for the individual categories in a variable do not add to the total base number because only an illustrative range of categories is included.

# List of tables

Table 2.1  Trade union recognition in establishments that closed        16
           down between 1984 and 1990

Table 2.2  Comparisons between establishments that closed between        17
           1984 and 1990 and all those existing in 1984

Table 2.3  Comparisons between the private sector in 1984 and            18
           establishments that had closed by 1990

Table 2.4  Size, sector, ownership and workforce composition of new      20
           workplaces, 1990

Table 2.5  Proportion of establishments with trade union recognition     23
           among all establishments and younger workplaces, by
           various characteristics, 1990

Table 2.6  Levels of decision-making within multi-establishment          25
           enterprises, 1990

Table 2.7  Level of management decision-making regarding trade           26
           union derecognition at the workplace in relation to current
           level of bargaining for  largest manual negotiating group,
           1990

Table 2.8  Level of management decision-making regarding trade           27
           union derecognition at the workplace in relation to current
           level of bargaining for largest non-manual negotiating
           group, 1990

Table 2.9  Level of management decision-making regarding trade           28
           union recognition at the workplace in relation to current
           level of pay determination for manual workers, 1990

Table 2.10 Level of management decision-making regarding trade           29
           union recognition at the workplace in relation to current
           level of pay determination for non-manual workers, 1990

Table 2.11 Extent of union recognition by age of establishment, 1980     30
           and 1990

Table 2.12 Degrees of union presence by various establishment            31
           characteristics, 1984 and 1990

Table 3.1   Proportion of workplaces with union members having a          39
            single union, 1990

Table 3.2   Proportion of workplaces in industry and commerce with        41
            any union members and with a single union with members,
            1990

Table 3.3   Characteristics of the ten unions most commonly involved      42
            in single union representation at workplace level, 1990

Table 3.4   The distribution of union membership density within           44
            single union and multi-union workplaces, 1990

Table 3.5   Types of employee in union membership within single          46
            union and multi-union workplaces, 1990

Table 3.6   Extent of union recognition among single union and           47
            multi-union workplaces, 1990

Table 3.7   Proportion of workplaces with different numbers of           48
            recognised unions, 1990

Table 3.8   Number of recognised unions, by age of workplace            49

Table 3.9   Proportion of employees covered by collective bargaining     52
            and union membership density in single and multi-union
            workplaces, 1990

Table 3.10  Presence of union representatives at single and multi-union  53
            workplaces, by age of workplace, 1990

Table 3.11  Existence of check-off arrangements at single and multi-     54
            union workplaces, by age of workplace, 1990

Table 4.1   The extent of formal sole union agreements in workplaces     57
            with a single recognised union, 1990

Table 4.2   Features of trade union representation in workplaces with a   60
            single recognised union, 1990

Table 4.3   Proportion of establishments with recognised unions for      61
            manual workers where each of six issues was negotiated
            with management, 1990

Table 4.4   Procedures for resolving pay disputes by type of union       64
            representation, 1990

Table 4.5   Constraints on management's ability to organise work in      68
            unionised workplaces, 1990

Table 4.6   Union constraints on management flexibility in relation to   69
            number of unions and number of negotaiting units, 1990

Table 4.7  Union constraints on management flexibility in single        71
           union workplaces, 1990

Table 4.8  Types of single union representation, 1990                    73

Table 5.1  The extent of consultative committees at workplace level     79
           in the union and non-union sectors, 1984 and 1990

Table 5.2  Indicators of the functioning of principal consultative      82
           committees among younger and older workplaces, 1990

Table 5.3  Methods used by management to communicate with or            85
           consult employees, 1984 and 1990

Table 5.4  The extent of regular meetings between junior managers       87
           and their subordinates, 1984 and 1990

Table 5.5  The extent of regular meetings between senior managers       89
           and all the workforce, 1984 and 1990

Table 5.6  Other methods used by managements to communicate with        92
           or consult employees, 1984 and 1990

Table 5.7  Communication methods in single union establishments,        94
           1990

Table 5.8  The amount of information given by management to             96
           employees or their representatives, by type of union
           representation, 1990

Table 5.9  Extent of employee financial participation schemes in        100
           industry and commerce, 1990, by type of enterprise

Table 5.10 Extent of employee financial participation schemes in        102
           industry and commerce, 1990, by workforce composition
           and trade union representation

Table 5.11 Indicators of 'single status' with respect to manual and     106
           non-manual workers, 1980 and 1990

Table 5.12 The extent of three features of common conditions of         108
           employment for manual and non-manual employees, 1990

Table 5.13 The extent of equal provision of (a) four fringe benefits    111
           and (b) seven indicators of 'single status' for manual and
           non-manual workers, 1990

Table 6.1  The extent of four features of the 'new style agreements'    126
           in 1990

Table A.1  Sampling fractions and numbers of census units drawn         137
           from the selected main samples, 1980, 1984 and 1990

Table A.2  Summary of fieldwork response for main samples, 1980,     144
          1984 and 1990

Table A.3  The selection and achievement of interviews with union    146
          representatives, 1990

Table A.4  Comparison by employment size, of sample after second     150
          weighting and estimated population, 1990

Table A.5  Addresses removed from the 'New Workplaces'               155
          Supplementary Sample listing prior to contacting

Table A.6  Addresses available for screening for the 'New            157
          Workplaces' Supplementary Sample

Table A.7  Addresses screened for the 'New Workplaces'               159
          Supplementary Sample

Table A.8  Comparison of the 'New Workplaces' Supplementary          162
          Sample with the 1990 WIRS main sample, by region and
          activity

Table A.9  Sampling errors and design factors for a selection of 1990  163
          survey variables

# 1 Introduction

There is now widespread agreement that the last decade saw a major transformation in British industrial relations. The decline in the role of trade unions and employers' associations, the reduction in collective activity by workers and the reassertion of managerial authority are widely regarded as historical fact by commentators, politicians, academics and the general public alike. The change has recently been summarised neatly, if simplistically, by a leading writer in the field under the title, 'The End of Institutional Industrial Relations'.[1] He went on to say, 'Partial surveys and case studies in the last decade have sought to describe and analyse these changes, but it is only now that we have the data to see how far things have changed since 1980 and to begin to explain why this is so and what the effects are.' The data referred to was that from the third Workplace Industrial Relations Survey[2] and the source for the article was the survey sourcebook,[3] published in 1992.

Our aim in this report is to shed further light on Britain's changing pattern of industrial relations, using that same highly detailed and comprehensive source of research data, the 1990 Workplace Industrial Relations Survey (WIRS) and the two earlier surveys in the series. The initial volume on the 1990 survey gave an overview of the most recent results. It also presented numerous comparisons with the two previous surveys. That broad picture of the changing pattern of structures and practices in the field of employment relations over the 1980s left many matters unexplored and it is one of the two starting points for the analysis presented in this volume. The other starting point was a growing perception from the mid 1980s onwards that management and industrial relations were experiencing an influx of new ideas and practices which might radically change the map of British employee relations if they were to become widespread. This led us to incorporate a number of new questions in the 1990 survey, designed to capture the extent of these novel practices and the types of workplace in which they were to be found. The overall results of many of these questions were included in our initial report on the survey, but it was left to this volume to explore the data in more detail and to give an overall account of the new practices.

## 'The new industrial relations'

The 'new industrial relations' covered three distinct patterns of employee relations arrangements, different from the patterns of the past. One of these was the 'Japanese model', exemplified by the Toshiba Consumer Products factory set up in Plymouth in 1981. The policies and practices introduced there attracted widespread publicity and a number of them were adopted, either as a package or piecemeal, elsewhere during the 1980s.[4] Core elements of the package were:

- sole bargaining rights for a single trade union;
- a 'no-strike' agreement with binding 'final offer' arbitration as a last resort in disputes of interest;
- a broadly based forum for consultation and employee participation;
- 'single status' conditions of employment; and
- complete freedom on the part of management to organise work.

Such arrangements aroused deep and lasting controversy within the trade union movement, particularly when their introduction involved competition between trade unions for the exclusive representation rights in prospect at new sites. The real extent of such arrangements is hard to judge.[5] But they may have, or have had, a wider importance, as Industrial Relations Services recently argued:

> The significance of the industrial relations procedures associated with single-union deals is far greater than the number of companies and employees covered would suggest. Their importance is symbolic; arguably, they provide a classic illustration of the style of industrial relations that management would *ideally* like to adopt... companies on existing 'brownfield' sites with more traditional industrial relations machinery may embrace the employment precedents set on single-union sites. We may thus be looking at the shape of the industrial relations agenda of the 1990s.[6]

The second version of 'the new industrial relations' involved not the 'comprehensive, single-union agreement' and its accompanying arrangements but the complete and continuing avoidance of trade union involvement. Union avoidance at new workplaces was far less controversial and thus attracted much less public attention. In many private sector industries, particularly those dominated by small independent firms, the absence of trade unions has always been the common pattern. But as yet we do not know whether union avoidance has become a more common feature of newer workplaces or if the processes of maturation that sometimes led to unionisation have been attenuated.

While newer workplaces are an obvious source of change, both as exemplars and in terms of their influence on the overall pattern of industrial relations in the economy, it is clear that they are not the only source. Older workplaces may adopt 'new industrial relations' practices if the benefits of doing so are generally recognised by those involved or if management are able to impose the necessary changes. Commentators and practitioners would probably agree that bringing such changes about in older workplaces is more difficult and time-consuming than making the arrangements from the start on a new site. But since older workplaces predominate in the economy, changes within them are at least as important a part of the overall picture as the arrangements adopted at new sites.

**'Human resource management'**
Alongside growing discussion of 'the new industrial relations' in the two forms mentioned above was an emerging interest among employers and managers in 'human resource management' (HRM). To some this offered the prospect of avoiding unions by kindness. Although variously used, often with evangelistic overtones, the term generally encompassed the following elements: managerial policies designed to engender employee commitment to managerial goals, employee flexibility in terms of the work or jobs performed, a general emphasis on quality in both outputs and processes and, finally, an integration of management's personnel (or 'human resource') policies with its strategic business planning.[7] The translation of these management policies into practice is an inherently problematic process. And gathering and interpreting research evidence on the existence of such policies or practices also has its problems. Nevertheless we have a number of questions in the WIRS series, and particularly in the most recent survey, which can provide indicators of some of the actual practices that would be expected to exist if HRM policies were implemented. Moreover, our evidence is uniquely well placed to discern in broad terms the types of workplaces and organisations in which they are apparent. We can see whether, for example, HRM techniques are largely confined to non-union situations, or are associated with 'new industrial relations' agreements, or have been adopted into situations with more traditional industrial relations arrangements. We can see to what extent they are predominantly a feature of newer workplaces or of foreign owned plants, as much of the literature suggests. In some instances we can use data from the 1980 survey to look at change over the decade and thus counter some of the bias that comes from focusing on the new and the newsworthy.

Thus the first main theme that runs through this book is encapsulated in the question 'is there a new industrial relations in Britain?' To the extent that the answer is positive we seek to see which of the three broad types of arrangement is predominant. Our second theme is more broadly based and addresses the issues of how and why.

To this latter question, two broadly alternative answers are possible. One would be that the influx of newer workplaces with the newer practices, plus the disappearance of older workplaces with traditional practices, was the main source of change. This we would label 'compositional' or structural change. The alternative answer would be that the main source of development was the changes in the practices and behaviour at workplaces existing throughout the period studied. This we label 'within-unit' change. Naturally these are these two types of explanation are not mutually exclusive in an absolute sense; but one type may appear from the evidence to have been more influential than the other.

The different elements of the WIRS datasets give us the ability to analyze these broadly opposing explanations of change. But although the various elements of the WIRS series are distinct, they have a number of common features with which readers will wish to be familiar before we go on to mention the main differences.

### The essential features of the WIRS design

The WIRS series has a number of key distinguishing characteristics. First of all, the establishment or workplace is the principal unit of analysis. By a 'workplace' this we mean an individual place of employment at a distinct address and encompassing the activities of a single employer. In order to provide stylistic variation we refer interchangeably in this report to workplaces, sites, units or establishments. When talking about manufacturing workplaces we also use the synonyms plant, factory or workshop. Most workplaces within the surveyed population belong to larger organisations, which we refer to variously as enterprises or businesses. Some of the WIRS questioning relates to these larger organisations, but the main focus is on the workplace.

A second key feature is the focus of the surveys on larger workplaces, where the more formal and structured relationships between management and employees that are the central concern of the series are most commonly found. Workplaces may range in size from those with a single employee to those employing several thousands. WIRS excludes the smallest of these, workplaces with less than 25 employees.[8]

Barring the exclusion of small workplaces, the coverage of the surveys is virtually comprehensive. Their scope includes all manufacturing industries, construction, extraction and all the service industries, both private and public. The only sizeable omissions are agriculture and coal mining, neither of which form a very substantial proportion of employment. In all, the surveys cover around 70 per cent of employees in Great Britain. The surveys consist of large, nationally representative samples of workplaces. The design incorporates rigorous statistical sampling and there is no clustering in the sample selection, since this might lead to under-representation of particular types of workplace. The sample sizes for the main surveys have exceeded 2000 in each wave in the series. In the main sector of employment to which our analysis in this volume is devoted – industry and commerce – the main samples are each in the region of 1500 cases.

The surveys use role-holders as key informants about their workplace. The main respondent in each case is the senior manager responsible for personnel or industrial relations matters, broadly defined. Other role-holders (worker representatives and other managers) provide additional information, although their reports are less relevant to this volume than the initial, overview volumes on the three surveys.[9] The great majority of our primary management respondents worked at the establishments about which they were interviewed.

The data were collected during the course of personal, face-to-face interviews carried out by professional interviewers specifically trained for the WIRS surveys and practised in the administration of complex and highly structured questionnaires. Considerable resources, both during and after fieldwork, were put into ensuring that the data were of high quality. A clear indication of the quality of the datasets is their high response rates. On the main 1990 survey this was 83 per cent. On the 'panel' dataset, to be discussed shortly, it was 87 per cent. In short, the WIRS series is the largest, most comprehensive and authoritative research resource on industrial relations and employee relations at workplace level.

This outline of the key features of the WIRS datasets applies, with few exceptions, to the series as a whole. We now turn to the different components in the overall series to set out the part that each component can play in our analysis in this volume.

**'Within-unit' change: the 1984-1990 panel sample**
The WIRS dataset that enables us to measure 'within-unit' change is the panel of workplaces interviewed in both 1984 and 1990. Where identical or comparable questions were used, we can with the panel dataset measure changes in either direction in those workplaces that existed at both points in time. This we have already done for a number of industrial relations characteristics in our earlier volume.[10] Two contrasting examples are worth recalling. In explaining the overall fall in the presence of

workplace-level joint consultative committees, our trading sector panel showed that just as many workplaces acquired such committees as had lost them.[11] Thus, in this example, 'within-unit' change balanced out and the overall fall in the presence of such committees was essentially compositional. By contrast, the decline in trade union recognition was partly, if not largely, explained by 'within-unit' change; we concluded this because our panel cases had a substantial preponderance of cases where recognition had been lost.

Hence our panel sample gives us a powerful tool for discriminating between the two major sources of change. But it has two important limitations. The most important is that the scope of the panel sample is limited to *industrial and commercial establishments,* the 'trading sector' of the economy. The non-trading public services (education, health, local and central government) were excluded as an economy measure because most of the interest in a panel dataset among potential users of it was concentrated on industry and commerce. In terms of our interest in 'the new industrial relations', the restriction is no great disadvantage. All of the 'new-style agreements' quoted in the literature were in private industry and commerce; none were in the public sector, largely because of the overwhelming centralisation of public sector industrial relations institutions and the near universality of collective bargaining. The second limitation of our panel sample is that no interviews with worker representatives were carried out in 1990 in panel cases, in contrast with the main 1990 WIRS sample. This imposes few limitations on the data available to us because virtually all the relevant questions were covered in the main management interviews.

**Compositional change**

In studying compositional change over the period covered by our panel, 1984 to 1990, we have not just one but fours datasets at our disposal. These are:

(a) the sample of 1984 industrial and commercial workplaces which had closed down by 1990 (derived from the panel element of the project),
(b) the 1984 main sample,
(c) the 1990 main sample, particularly the survey questions on the age of workplaces,
(d) the separate 1990 sample of 'new workplaces'.

The role of each of these datasets in our analysis merits some preliminary remarks.

## The sample of panel closures

The first of these datasets arises enable us to measure how important the 'deaths' of workplaces are in the disappearance or declining incidence of 'the old industrial relations'. The sample arises from the fact that not all of the workplaces in our 1984 sample still existed by the time we approached them for an interview in 1990. Having identified workplaces that closed, but did not move their activities to another site, we can examine their characteristics as recorded in 1984.[12] By comparing these 'closures' with the relevant part of the main 1984 sample (item b, above) we have one element of the picture of compositional change over the period 1984 to 1990. Some 10 per cent of establishments in our 1984 trading sector sample had closed down by 1990, implying an average annual rate of closure of between one and two per cent.

## Younger workplaces in the 1990 main sample

In the most recent survey in the WIRS series our question about the age of workplaces in the sample sought as much precision in the response as we thought was reasonable.[13] Our management respondents were asked, 'for how long has this establishment (workplace) been operating here at this address?' The answer was coded to individual years for up to 20 years, but with a single code for those over 20 years. Having this detailed measure of age for workplaces up to 20 years old means that we can examine one of the important, unanswered questions about change in industrial relations: does the mere passage of time increase the tendency for workplaces to acquire the formal practices and institutions which characterise 'the old industrial relations'?[14]

Our more detailed question on the age of workplaces also means that we can identify those that were six years old or less, in other words ones established from 1984 onwards. In fact, 22 per cent of our sample of industrial and commercial establishments were 'younger workplaces' within this definition, indicating a substantial degree of change in the composition of the productive part of the economy.

It would be wrong, however, to think of all of these workplaces as having been born *de novo* from 1984 onwards. This is because workplaces may come into existence – or, more precisely, come into the scope of the WIRS sample – in a number of ways. The principal distinction to be made is between workplaces that were created at sites where there had previously been no such activity and workplaces that arose from a transfer of activity by the employer from another site. Our question asked, where the workplace was 20 years old or less, whether it had 'always been here' or 'had a previous address'. The former cases can be thought of as being *original workplaces,* as against *movers* which are the latter.[15]

Of the 'younger workplaces' in our 1990 main sample, 29 per cent were new, original workplaces, while the remainder were movers. Thus movers constitute the clear majority of younger workplaces and have a greater quantitative impact on the changing picture than new original workplaces. This is potentially a major source of change. For if employers treat the move as an opportunity to set up a completely new system of employee relations practices, such as they would on a greenfield site, then movers would account for much of the compositional change in the overall picture of employee relations practices that we observe. If, on the other hand, institutions and practices are transferred from the old site to the new site in a move then movers would account for none of the change in the overall picture. Broadly speaking the latter situation seems more likely if the workplace belongs to an organisation with centralised and uniform arrangements, such as are common among multiple retailers, high street banks and some other service industries. Yet there are well known examples of the converse case where employers have moved operations largely in order to institute completely new employee relations practices at the new site.[16] But what the general tendency is among workplaces that move is an empirical question which, to date, has received no general answer.

Two characteristics of movers seemed to us to be generally relevant to the possible transfer of practices from the old site to the new one. These were the proportion of the workforce transferred and the distance involved. The answers to those questions revealed that the typical move within the last 20 years involved a transfer of well over three quarters of the former workforce from the old site to the new one and a distance of under two miles. Neither of these features varied in any clear pattern in relationship to size, ownership, industry and so on; the circumstances surrounding the move and the degree to which the previous workforce was transferred appeared to be unrelated to the matters covered by our inquiry. However, younger workplaces were a little different in these two respects. If anything, they tended to have moved a shorter distance and a taken a higher proportion of their workforces with them. The typical move, then, does not involve a radical break in the composition of the workforce which would create the opportunity for a 'clean break' in employment practices and employee relations arrangements.

Although the question remains an empirical one – and one which we shall address at various points in the course of our analysis – for the moment it seems more likely that movers typically retain many if not most of their employee relations arrangements during the course of moving from one site to another.

As a consequence we should, at least initially, conceive of newer workplaces as excluding movers. Treated in this way, our results suggest that over the last 20 years the rate of formation – or 'births' – of workplaces currently having 25 or more employees has averaged about 1 per cent per year.[17] On this basis, the scope for this element of compositional change to have a major impact on the overall changes observed seems relatively small.

There are, however, two respects in which we are under-estimating the full extent of the youngest workplaces in the population. This under-estimation arises from the fact that our sampling frame for the 1990 main survey was, inevitably, somewhat out of date when it was used, being based on information relating to September 1987. We attempted to remedy this by designing a separate sample of 'new workplaces', using an alternative selection procedure.

### The 1990 sample of 'new workplaces'

The separate sample of 'new workplaces' was designed to cover new, original workplaces set up after September 1987, and workplaces that had grown on their current site from under 25 employees in September 1987 to 25 or more in 1990.[18] The results of this venture are fully described in Appendix B. The upshot is that, while we have what appears to be a plausibly representative sample of the workplaces we were aiming to obtain, the sample is small. It contains 84 cases in total, of which 75 are in industry and commerce. Of the latter, there were 40 cases of new, original workplaces established since 1987, and 15 cases which were older but had grown from below our 25 employee threshold in 1987 to above it in 1990. The remainder were movers which had also grown from below to above our size threshold.

Besides the smallness of the supplementary sample and each of its three constituent categories there is a second difficulty, which is in estimating the size of the population to which it relates. As a consequence, we consider it inadvisable to simply add the 'new workplaces' sample to the main sample – with some appropriate weighting scheme – and treat the combined dataset as representing the population of workplaces with at least 25 employees in 1990. We are therefore obliged to adopt an alternative treatment, which is to use the 'new workplaces' sample as an adjunct to our analysis of the main sample according to the age of workplaces. Used in this way, the supplementary sample of 'new workplaces' can still contribute significantly to our analysis of the part played by the changing composition of workplaces in the economy.

To summarise, our further analysis of the changing pattern of industrial relations in Britain – and the possible emergence of a distinctive pattern of 'new industrial relations' – is focused exclusively on workplaces in industry and commerce. Most attention will be given to the period 1984 to 1990, for which all of the above-mentioned datasets are directly relevant, although we shall also look more broadly at the age of workplaces. But we concentrate on the more recent period because if there are clues to the future development of industrial relations in the past, it is surely here that we are most likely to find them.

### The nature and contents of the book
We have used detailed tabular analysis to explore the results of the three surveys in the WIRS series for the purposes of this report. That method of analysis was adopted for three main reasons. It provided results that could be presented in an understandable way to a general readership. It allowed us to use the various datasets, mentioned above, in a way that readily accommodated their different sizes and complexities. And it enabled us to cover a large number of survey questions and variables relevant to the broad-ranging interest of our inquiry. Such a method inevitably leaves unanswered questions about the precise impact of different characteristics upon particular matters of interest. We have no doubt that a great number of more sharply focused questions about the nature of British industrial relations can be addressed with the WIRS data, often in combination with more sophisticated statistical methods. Such analyses have already burgeoned on the basis of the earlier surveys and work-in-progress on the 1990 survey is beginning to emerge.[19] We intend to contribute to that literature too. But the broad purpose of the current report is most readily met by the type of analysis presented.

Tabular analysis of survey data is, in any case, more complicated in the case of surveys of workplaces that it is in the much more familiar case of surveys of individuals. This added complexity arises from three distinct sources. The first is that there are two alternative bases of description. In describing the extent of 'briefing groups', for example, one could use the *proportion of workplaces* with briefing groups, or one could use the *proportion of employees in workplaces* with briefing groups. These proportions can be substantially different because a small proportion of large workplaces employ a large proportion of employees: in our 1990 trading sector sample, for example, larger workplaces (those employing 500 or more people) made up only 2 per cent of the establishments, but they accounted for 21 per cent of employees covered by the survey. Presenting each of our survey results both on the basis of workplaces and on the basis of employees would be time-consuming and tedious. But in cases where the particular practice of interest applies only to some employees, as it often does, the proportion of employees in workplaces with that practice could be misinterpreted; it could be mistaken for the proportion of employees covered by that practice. For example, many fewer employees are actually covered by collective bargaining than are employed in workplaces where collective bargaining occurs, as we know from further, more detailed questioning. In general, therefore, this report presents analysis based upon *workplaces* as the principal unit of analysis. That follows the general practice adopted in the earlier volumes on the WIRS series.

The second source of complexity in surveys of workplaces is that there may be distinct sub-units of the workplace which have their own arrangements and need separate questioning to uncover this. An obvious example is that manual workers and white-collar staff may have separate or different arrangements. This makes it more difficult to summarise the general picture of those arrangements for employees in general, but it makes it possible to investigate within-establishment differences – as we do in Chapter 5 with regard to 'single status' employment conditions.

A third source of possible complexity in surveys of workplaces is that there may be more than one respondent providing information on any given workplace. Multiple respondents are a feature of the WIRS series and one of its strengths. That feature was exploited most fully in Daniel's analysis of the 1984 survey questions on the introduction of technical and organisational change.[20] Our initial volume on the 1990 survey also devoted substantial sections to the responses of worker representatives. In this volume, however, the matters of interest were almost entirely covered only in the interviews with our main management respondent. The added complexity of reporting multiple-respondent data is therefore unnecessary in the analysis presented.

The structure of the report is as follows. In Chapter 2 we explore the sources of change that led to the substantial decline in the representation of employees by trade unions since 1984: the growth in 'non-unionism'. In Chapter 3 we look at the extent and nature of single union representation, as a main element of the package deals that constituted the trade union related version of 'the new industrial relations'. Chapter 4 explores single union agreements in detail. Chapter 5 examines some of the remaining features of the new-style arrangements and a number of HRM-style practices which might form part of an alternative model of employee relations. We summarise the analysis in Chapter 6 and draw out some of its implications for the future of employee relations in Britain.

**Notes and references**

1. John Purcell, 'The End of Institutional Industrial Relations', *Political Quarterly,* vol.64, no.1, 1993, pp.6-23.

2. The ED/ESRC/PSI/ACAS Workplace Industrial Relations Surveys, to give them their full title, are sponsored by the Employment Department, the Economic and Social Research Council, the Policy Studies Institute (with funds from the Leverhulme Trust) and the Advisory, Conciliation and Arbitration Service. Surveys were undertaken in 1980, 1984 and 1990.

3. Neil Millward, David Smart, Mark Stevens and W R Hawes, *Workplace Industrial Relations in Transition: the ED/ESRC/PSI/ACAS Surveys,* Dartmouth Publishing, Aldershot, 1992.

4. Philip Bassett, *Strike Free,* Macmillan, London, 1986; L. Rico, 'The new industrial relations: British electricians' new-style agreements', *Industrial and Labor Relations Review,* vol.41, no.1, October 1987, pp.63-78; Malcolm Trevor, *Toshiba's New British Company,* Policy Studies Institute, London, 1988; see particularly pp.221-42, 'Toshiba as a model'.

5. Following earlier case-study material, assessments of the numbers and types of single-union agreements have been given by Industrial Relations Services; see their *IRS Employment Trends* No.523, November 1992, pp.6-15; No.528, January 1993, pp.3-15; No.529, February 1993, pp.4-12.

6. Industrial Relations Services, 1992, op.cit.

7. David Guest, 'Human resource management: its implications for industrial relations and trade unions' in J. Storey (ed.) *New Perspectives on Human Resource Management,* Routledge, London, 1989.

8. The one exception to this rule is in the 1984-1990 panel sample, in which workplaces with less than 25 employees at the time of interview in 1990 were included.

9. Neil Millward et al., 1992, op.cit. for the 1990 survey; Neil Millward and Mark Stevens, *British Workplace Industrial Relations 1980-1984,* Gower, Aldershot, 1986, for the 1984 survey; W W Daniel and Neil Millward, *Workplace Industrial Relations in Britain,* Heinemann Educational Books, London, 1983, for the 1980 survey.

10. Neil Millward et al. (1992), op.cit. See index entries listed under *panel data* on p.392.

11. Neil Millward et al. (1992), op.cit., pp.153-4.

12. The 87 cases in the 'panel unproductives' dataset consisted of 70 cases classified as 'closed down', 'derelict/vacant/demolished' or 'no trace of address' and a further 17 that were no longer present at the sampled address. The latter 17 included 4 that had been amalgamated with another address in the sample and 2 that were classified by interviewers as 'known to have moved but no trace of new address' or 'assumed to have moved'. All these 17 have been treated as closures for present purposes.

Further analysis to investigate whether this is a reasonable procedure would be desirable.

13. Our approach was probably too cautious. A useful distinction between establishments aged 20 to 49 years old and those over 50 years old could probably have been used, given the experience of the Australian Workplace Industrial Relations Survey: Ron Callus, Alison Morehead, Mark Cully and John Buchanan, *Industrial Relations at Work,* Australian Government Publishing Service, Canberra, 1991.

14. 'We have very little evidence on the impact of aging on HRM or industrial relations'. David Guest and Patrice Rosenthal, 'Industrial Relations in Greenfield Sites', Centre for Economic Performance, London School of Economics, Discussion Paper No.127, 1992.

15. More complicated cases involve establishments that result from the amalgamation of two or more establishments (of the same employer) and, alternatively, those that came about from the splitting up of what was previously a single establishment. Although both types of case did occur in our sample, they were not identified by further questioning, the expected numbers being very small. However, cases of this sort were dealt with by interviewers using more detailed instructions on how to identify eligible establishments deriving from their original, issued addresses.

16. Philip Bassett, op.cit., 1986.

17. 20 per cent of the 1990 sample of industrial and commercial establishments were 20 years old or less and had been set up on their current site.

18. It also included, for the sake of completeness, a particular type of mover, ones which had had less than 25 employees in September 1987 and had 25 or more employees in 1990.

19. A register of working papers and publications arising from the WIRS series is to be established by the WIRS User Group, administered by the ESRC Data Archive at the University of Essex. The forerunner of this register was published in 1992: Neil Millward, *A Bibliography of Analyses based on the British Workplace Industrial Relations Surveys,* Policy Studies Institute, London.

20. W W Daniel, *Workplace Industrial Relations and Technical Change,* Frances Pinter and the Policy Studies Institute, London, 1987. The findings have recently been updated on the basis of the 1990 survey. See W W Daniel and Neil Millward, 'Findings from the Workplace Industrial Relations Surveys' in Jon Clark (ed.) *Human Resource Management and Technical Change,* Sage Publications, London.

# 2 The collective representation of employees

The first issue to be addressed in our analysis is the decline in the collective representation of employees during the 1980s, to which we drew attention in the earlier volume. We have a number of possible measures of the representation of employees by trade unions and it will be useful for this and later chapters if we establish a clear terminlogy.

In the broadest sense the potential for an employee to be represented by a trade union in his or her dealings with management is created by the act of joining a union. A union member may call upon an official of the union for assistance in a grievance or dispute at the worklace or to present his or her view on work-related matters to management. There is, however, no general obligation in law on the employer to meet or accept communication from a union official attempting to act on behalf of an employee, which is why the minimal implication of membership is only *potential* representation. However, this potential, plus the fact that trade unions do have the right of representation in industrial tribunals adjudicating cases of possible unfair dismissal (and other specific circumstances), makes it reasonable to regard the mere *presence of union members at a workplace* as a minimal degree of employee representation by trade unions. Focusing on the workplace as the unit of analyis we thus regard 'union presence' as indicating a minimal degree of employee representation by a union or unions, or 'union representation' for short.

Employers and managers may allow a trade union to represent its members on certain matters as a matter of normal practice. For example, the employer may have a formal procedure which an agrieved employee can invoke if he or she feels unfairly or wrongly treated and may grant the trade union the right to represent its members at a certain stage of the procedure. Or in a workplace with some form of consultative forum the employer may allow union members to choose some of the employee representatives. Again it is reasonable to regard such arrangements as a form of 'union representation'.

An employer may go beyond this and accord a trade union the status of a partner in jointly agreeing, or negotiating, certain matters in relation to its members at the workplace. In such circumstances the employer *recognises* the union for the purpose of collective bargaining. A workplace in which there are union members and the management has granted their trade union such a role can be termed one that has 'recognised unions' or has 'union recognition'. However, the bargaining or negotiation may cover one or more of any number of matters that impinge upon employees, some of which may be relatively trivial. It is widely accepted that some the most crucial issues for employees are the terms and conditions of their employment and in particular their pay. It is *where pay and conditions of employment are jointly agreed between management and trade unions* that we talk in this report, as in all our reports on the WIRS series, of full 'union recognition'. Later, towards the end of this chapter we introduce an intermediate definition of union representation which we term 'partial recognition'. But generally throughout this report union recognition means the state of affairs where management has accorded the union or unions the privilege of representing its members in negotiations over pay and conditions of employment.

It was the decline in the extent of union recognition – the proportion of workplaces with a trade union or unions recognised by management in the sense defined above – that we highlighted in the initial report on the 1990 survey. That measure fell in industry and commerce from 52 per cent to 40 per cent of workplaces. How did this change come about? Was it the result of the changing composition of industry and commerce or of a change in the behaviour of managements in relation to trade unions? What gave rise to the dramatic increase in 'non-unionism'?

**Plant closures**
We begin by looking at the closure of workplaces. If workplaces that ceased operating between 1984 and 1990 were predominantly ones with recognised unions, then this could account for part of the fall from 52 to 40 per cent over the period. In fact, there was no such tendency. If anything, workplaces that closed down were somewhat *less* likely to have recognised unions in 1984 than the generality of workplaces in the trading sector. The proportions were 52 per cent for all workplaces and 49 per cent for those that subsequently closed (see Table 2.1). If closures had been the only source of change in the extent of union recognition, the 1990 figure would have been slightly higher, not markedly lower.

On the surface, this seems a surprising result, given earlier findings from the WIRS series. Changes in the extent of union recognition between 1980 and 1984 certainly seemed to be partly accounted for by the closure of large manufacturing workplaces where recognition was extremely common.[1] But the period 1984 to 1990 did not contain an economic recession that

**Table 2.1    Trade union recognition in establishments that closed down between 1984 and 1990**

*Percentages*

|  | All establishments in 1984 | Establishments that closed down between 1984 and 1990 |
|---|---|---|
| Proportion of establishments with any recognised trade unions | 52 | 49 |
| Base: industrial and commercial establishments specified in column headings | | |
| *Unweighted* | *1385[1]* | *87[2]* |
| *Weighted* | *1373* | *138* |

1.    Source:    1984 WIRS main sample.
2.    Source:    1984-1990 WIRS panel sample, unproductive cases.

particularly affected manufacturing industry, whereas the earlier period had. Moveover, the evidence for the explanation for the earlier period was more inferential, relying on just the two cross-sectional surveys and a very small panel sample. Here we have much more direct evidence on compositional change, being able to isolate the part played by plant closures. We can be confident that it was not plant closures that led to the decline in the extent of union recognition in the period 1984 to 1990.

The explanation of this surprising finding is of some interest and will be useful in our subsequent analysis of whether closures contributed to changes in other industrial relations characteristics. In short, although workplaces that closed after 1984 had some characteristics that were positively associated with union recognition, they also had others that were negatively related to it. The two sets of effects appear to have roughly cancelled each other out. Tables 2.2 and Table 2.3 give the main results.

In Table 2.2 we see that closures were more common among workplaces in manufacturing industry, among nationalised industries or other state enterprises and among branches of larger firms rather than independent, single-plant firms. These three characteristics are all positively associated with union recognition. However, closures were more common among smaller workplaces: the average size of closures was 82 employees compared with 104 for all industrial and commercial establishments. Smaller workplaces are much less likely to have recognised unions.

Table 2.3 gives further results for the private sector only – that is, excluding state-owned enterprises. It shows that closures are less common

**Table 2.2   Comparisons between establishments that closed between 1984 and 1990 and all those existing in 1984**

|  | All establishments in 1984 | Establishments that closed down between 1984 and 1990 |
|---|---|---|
|  |  | *Percentages* |
| **Sector** |  |  |
| Manufacturing | 31 | 41 |
| Services | 69 | 59 |
| **Ownership** |  |  |
| Private sector | 92 | 89 |
| Public sector | 8 | 11 |
| Branch of larger firm | 63 | 72 |
| Head office of larger firm | 11 | 12 |
| Independent establishment | 26 | 16 |
| **Size of establishment (employees)** |  |  |
| 25-49 | 51[1] | 55 |
| 50-99 | 27 | 26 |
| 100-499 | 20 | 17 |
| 500 or more | 3 | 1 |
|  |  | *Means* |
| Average size | 104 | 82 |

Base: industrial and commercial establishments specified in column headings

| | | |
|---|---|---|
| *Unweighted* | *1385*[2] | *87*[3] |
| *Weighted* | *1373* | *138* |

1.   See Note C.
2.   Source: 1984 WIRS main sample.
3.   Source: 1984-1990 WIRS panel sample, unproductive cases.

among trusts, charities, friendly societies, companies limited by guarantee, partnerships and self-proprietorships – all of these types of organisation are less likely to have recognised trade unions. Their relative permanence compared with workplaces belonging to limited companies (which are generally larger) would, if anything, suggest a decline in union recognition. So would the next characteristic shown, financial performance. Workplaces rated by our management respondents as performing below average for their industry in 1984 were twice as likely to have closed by 1990 as the generality of workplaces. Similar relationships held with a

**Table 2.3   Comparisons between the private sector in 1984 and establishments that had closed by 1990**

|  | All private sector establishments | Establishments that closed down between 1984 and 1990 |
|---|---|---|
|  |  | *Column percentages* |
| **Ownership** |  |  |
| Limited company, PLC | 86[1] | 98 |
| Trust, Friendly Society, Charity, Company Limited by guarantee | 7 | - |
| Partnership, self-proprietorship | 6 | 1 |
| Cooperative | 2 | 1 |
| **Financial performance** |  |  |
| Above average | 41 | 29 |
| Average | 41 | 39 |
| Below average | 6 | 12 |
| Not stated | 12 | 17 |
|  |  | *Means* |
| Mean of factors | 0.4 | − 0.4 |
|  |  | *Column percentages* |
| **Age of establishment in 1984** |  |  |
| Less than 5 years | 8 | 4 |
| 5 to 9 years | 13 | 21 |
| 10-24 | 28 | 33 |
| 25 | 48 | 42 |
| Not answered | 2 | - |

Base: private sector establishments specified in column headings.

| | | |
|---|---|---|
| *Unweighted* | *1189[2]* | *73[3]* |
| *Weighted* | *1267* | *123* |

1. See Note C.
2. Source: 1984 WIRS main sample.
3. Source: 1984-1990 WIRS panel sample, unproductive cases.

number of other economic indicators such as lack of sales growth, falling employment and below-capacity working. All these characteristics are more common among workplaces with recognised unions; they too would point towards closures being more common in unionised workplaces. But the final section of Table 2.3 points somewhat in the opposite direction.

This shows that closures were not concentrated among the oldest workplaces, but rather more among those of young to middle age. And recognised unions were much more common among the older workplaces that were more likely to have survived.

Overall, then, it was the smaller size and, to a lesser extent, the relative youth of workplaces that closed after 1984 that counteracted other characteristics which predisposed unionised establishments to have a higher rate of closure.[2] Positive and negative 'effects' appear to have largely cancelled out, with the net result we began with, namely, that closures made no contribution to the overall drop in union recognition between 1984 and 1990.

A similar picture emerged when we looked at our more detailed, employee-based measure of the influence of recognised unions. The proportion of employees covered by collective bargaining between unions and management registered a sharp fall between 1984 and 1990: from an average of 58 per cent to 43 per cent. But none of this fall was an effect of closures. Establishments that closed between 1984 and 1990 had on average 55 per cent of their employees covered by collective bargaining. The distribution of coverage among closures almost exactly matched that of the whole trading sector in 1984. So on this measure, too, none of the change between 1984 and 1990 can be attributed to closures.

An identical finding emerged with regard to our third main measure of the presence of trade unions – union membership density. Aggregate density fell from 50 per cent in 1984 to 39 per cent in 1990.[3] But establishments that closed had very similar levels of membership as the whole 1984 trading sector sample. Indeed, the aggregate level was identical, at 50 per cent. Again we can be sure that closures contributed nothing to the overall change between 1984 and 1990.

## The characteristics of younger workplaces

The other part of compositional change that is relevant to our investigation of the decline in collective representation since 1984 is the emergence of new workplaces in the population between 1984 and 1990. If these had less extensive collective representation, this could account for part of the overall decline. Here we have two sources of evidence: those workplaces in the 1990 main sample that had been established in 1984 or thereafter; and the supplementary sample of new workplaces set up since late 1987. As we explained in Chapter 1, more weight should be given to the former than the latter. For present purposes, movers are excluded from these younger workplaces, so we are confining our attention to original new workplaces or, more briefly, 'new workplaces'. As a preliminary to our

**Table 2.4  Size, sector, ownership and workforce composition of new
workplaces, 1990**

| | All trading sector | Original new workplaces estab. 1984 onwards | Original new workplaces estab. 1987 onwards |
|---|---|---|---|
| | | | *Column percentages* |
| **Size of workplace** | | | |
| 25-49 | 52 | 54 | 39[1] |
| 50-99 | 26 | 30 | 32 |
| 100-199 | 13 | 11 | 15 |
| 200-499 | 7 | 4 | 15 |
| 500-999 | 1 | 1 | - |
| 1000+ | 1 | * | - |
| | | | *Means* |
| Average size | 96 | 77 | 106 |
| | | | *Percentages* |
| **Sector** | | | |
| Manufacturing | 29 | 13 | 10 |
| Services | 71 | 87 | 90 |
| High technology industry | 6 | 9 | 2 |
| **Ownership** | | | |
| Private sector | 97 | 99 | 95 |
| State owned | 3 | 1 | 5 |
| Branch of larger firm | 68 | 82 | 83 |
| Head office of larger firm | 4 | 1 | 5 |
| Independent establishment | 28 | 17 | 12 |
| Foreign owned UK | 9 | 13 | 7 |
| multi-national | 31 | 23 | 29 |
| | | | *Means* |
| **Workforce composition** | | | |
| Percentage manual | 54 | 59 | 49 |
| Percentage of manual skilled | 30 | 21 | 12 |
| Percentage female | 38 | 50 | 55 |
| Percentage part-time | 14 | 28 | 32 |
| Base:  establishments in industry and commerce | | | |
| *Unweighted* | *1510[2]* | *74[2]* | *41[3]* |
| *Weighted* | *1452* | *91* | *41* |

1.  See Note C.
2.  Source: 1990 WIRS main sample.
3.  Source: supplementary sample of new workplaces, 1990-91.

discussion of trade union recognition we show in Table 2.4 how these new workplaces differed from the general population of workplaces in 1990. New (original) workplaces were somewhat smaller than the general population, as might be expected. Their average size in the main sample was 77 employees compared with 96 overall. The small supplementary sample shows a slightly larger average size, but this data hardly outweighs the more reliable finding from the main sample.

Both our samples of workplaces showed that many fewer of them were in manufacturing industry; the great preponderance (approaching 90 per cent) were in services. Retail distribution and hotels and catering were the service sectors with especially large numbers of new establishments. Banking, insurance and finance had very few. High technology industries, [4] most of which are in manufacturing, were not prominent.

New workplaces were considerably more likely to be part of larger organisations than independent, single-establishment firms. There was no marked tendency for them to be foreign owned, but UK firms that had no overseas subsidiaries appeared more active in setting up new workplaces than UK-based multinational companies. This might simply reflect the concentration of new workplaces in retailing and catering.

Table 2.4 shows four characteristics of workforce composition, some of which show substantial differences between new workplaces and the general population. Although new workplaces employed similar proportions of manual workers, substantially fewer of those manual workers were categorised as skilled. More than twice as many employees worked part time and, reflecting this, more of them were female.

There were some noteworthy associations with features of the workplace's environment. New (original) workplaces were more likely to be serving local markets and to be in markets with a substantial number of competitors. They were no more likely to be in travel-to-work areas with higher unemployment.

Intriguingly, markedly more managers in new workplaces rated the financial performance of their workplace to be below the average for their industry.

**Union recognition in younger workplaces**
Many of the features of new workplaces mentioned above are associated with non-unionism and it should be no surprise that fewer new workplaces had recognised trade unions than was generally the case. Only 29 per cent of workplaces established since 1984 had recognised unions, compared with 40 per cent for all workplaces in 1990. In our supplementary sample

of workplaces established since late 1987 the proportion was also lower (32 per cent).

Movers also had a much lower rate of recognition than older workplaces. For them the proportion in our main sample was 26 per cent. There seems little doubt that the characteristics of original new workplaces contributed to their lower rate of recognition. They were generally smaller, much more likely to be in the service sector (especially retailing and hotels and catering where union representation is particularly unusual), had fewer skilled workers (who have higher union membership) and had much higher proportions of part-time employees. In fact, the only characteristic shown in Table 2.4 that predisposes a workplace towards union recognition, but was more common among new workplaces, was being a branch of a larger organisation. This appears to be outweighed by the fact that the growth points in the economy contain a disproportionate amount of the types of workplace where union recognition has always been less common.

Direct evidence on effect of establishment age on the extent of recognition is broadly summarised in Table 2.5, using a number of dimensions. Because of the small number of original new workplaces these results also include movers and thus refer to all 'younger workplaces'. From the table it is apparent that the lower rate of recognition among younger workplaces is confined to establishments that belong to larger organisations; among single independent establishments there is no significant difference. However, along all the other dimensions shown in the table younger workplaces have a lower rate of recognition than is the case for the whole sample.[5] The underlying causes of this difference would seem to be quite general.

But while we have established that union recognition was less common among younger workplaces, the above analysis leaves a number of questions unanswered. We still know little about how recognition comes to be granted by managements to trade unions. Indeed, given that recognising trade unions is now entirely voluntary, and has been since 1980 under British law, those who believe that recognising a trade union always imposes costs on employers must wonder why nearly a third of workplaces established since 1984 have acquired this burden! We have a number of pieces of evidence from the 1990 survey which help illuminate this question.

First of all, we have the results of a direct question about how recent cases of formal recognition had come about. We asked managers about the largest manual union or group of unions at the workplace that was recognised; similar questions were asked in respect of non-manual unions. Because we felt that it would be difficult to give an account of how

**Table 2.5** **Proportion of establishments with trade union recognition among all establishments and younger workplaces, by various characteristics, 1990**

*Percentages*

| | All trading sector | Younger workplaces |
|---|---|---|
| All establishments | 40 | 27 |
| Part of larger organisation | 48 | 27 |
| Independent establishment | 21 | (27) |
| UK owned | 38 | 27 |
| Foreign owned | 37 | (23) |
| Manufacturing | 45 | 29 |
| Services | 38 | 26 |
| **Size of establishment** | | |
| 25-99 employees | 35 | 23 |
| 100-499 employees | 57 | 44 |
| 500 or more employees | 77 | (49) |
| **Proportion of workforce female** | | |
| 70 per cent or more | 34 | (31) |
| 30 to 70 per cent | 33 | 20 |
| Less than 30 per cent | 46 | 35 |
| **Proportion of workforce in ethnic minorities** | | |
| More than 10 per cent | 26 | (7) |
| 10 per cent or less | 38 | 30 |
| Base: establishments specified in column headings | | |
| *Unweighted* | *1510* | *267* |
| *Weighted* | *1452* | *316* |

Source: 1990 main sample.

recognition had come about if it was only informally agreed, we asked managers only in cases where there was a formal written agreement to recognise the union or unions. We further restricted the question to cases where recognition had been granted in the last six years. Even in these cases managers found the question difficult to answer and there were much higher than normal numbers of vague or missing responses. Moreover, because recognition was so much less common in younger workplaces, we had very few of these cases in which the question was asked. The few responses that we did have came into just two of the nine possible categories that we coded.

These were: *after discussion or negotiation between management and the unions,* and *by extension from elsewhere in the organisation.* The second of these was the more common. Thus although there certainly were cases of management conceding union recognition under pressure from union members, the more common occurrence, in these rare cases where there was a formal written recognition agreement in younger workplaces, was for management to offer or initiate union recognition to conform with its arrangements elsewhere in the organisation.

A further feature of union recognition in younger workplaces was the degree of informality compared with older workplaces. Our question on whether or not recognition of manual unions was written into a formal agreement revealed that for the 1990 sample as a whole three quarters of workplaces with union recognition for manual workers had a formal recognition agreement. But among younger workplaces this proportion was only a third. For non-manual unions the proportion for the whole sample was over 90 per cent; but for younger workplaces it was well under a half.[6] This gives us an initial and important result about the 'new industrial relations'. Formal agreements recognising trade unions were unusual in younger workplaces, even in those relatively few cases where the unions had gained recognition. Formal 'single union agreements' must be even less common, as we shall see in the next chapter.

**Employer policy on union recognition**
Our second strand of evidence about the process by which trade unions achieve recognition comes from new questions in the 1990 survey about the level of decision making on a small number of important issues that managements might have to decide from time to time. These questions were put to managers in establishments that belonged to multi-establishment enterprises, comprising 72 per cent of the sample. The three issues were the appointment of a senior manager, recognition or derecognition of a trade union or unions, and the use of any financial or budgetary surplus. The responses varied from *a decision would be made at this workplace* to *the decision would be made at Head Office.*[7] Table 2.6 gives the overall results from these three questions.

In comparison with the other two important issues, trade union recognition or derecognition was more frequently reported as being a head office matter. A half of respondents said that it would be decided at head office level compared with a quarter for decisions about senior managerial appointments and just over a third for the use of a financial surplus. A further quarter of workplaces were subject to intermediate level decisions or higher-level approval on recognition issues. In only a quarter of cases

**Table 2.6  Levels of decision-making within multi-establishment enterprises, 1990**

*Column percentages*

|  | Issue: | | |
|---|---|---|---|
|  | Union recognition or derecognition | Appointment of Senior Manager | Use of financial services |
| Workplace decision | 26[1] | 31 | 26 |
| Workplace recommendation and intermediate level approval | 3 | 8 | 6 |
| Intermediate level decision | 4 | 17 | 12 |
| Workplace recommendation and head office approval | 11 | 16 | 15 |
| Head office decision | 50 | 25 | 37 |
| Not answered | 5 | 3 | 3 |

Base: trading sector establishments belonging to multi-establishment enterprises.

| | | | |
|---|---|---|---|
| *Unweighted* | *1271* | *1271* | *1271* |
| *Weighted* | *1039* | *1039* | *1039* |

1.  See Note C.

did establishment managers report that they had autonomy on the question of union recognition. It is hard to avoid the conclusion that trade union recognition was felt by corporate management to be such an important issue that it could not be left in the hands of establishment-level management in the great majority of cases.

There are probably numerous reasons for this highly centralised treatment of the issue of trade union recognition, but the most plausible one is the perceived importance to corporate management of an individual establishment conforming to the system of pay determination adopted in the enterprise. If pay is determined unilaterally by management in all the establishments of an enterprise, the repercussions of an individual workplace recognising a trade union are likely to be crucial and widespread. Similarly, where there is enterprise-wide bargaining the consequences of an individual workplace derecognising its trade unions would also be of considerable import, even in current legal conditions where coordinated trade union opposition to such a move is highly circumscribed. Broadly speaking, multi-establishment companies either have recognised unions in all their establishments or in none of them,[8] so decisions to break with this policy would be major ones.

**Table 2.7** **Level of management decision-making regarding trade union derecognition at the workplace in relation to current level of bargaining for largest manual negotiating group, 1990**

*Column percentages*

| | Most important bargaining level: | | |
| | Establishment | Enterprise | Multi-employer |
| --- | --- | --- | --- |
| **Level of decision on derecognition** | | | |
| Establishment decision | 34 | 8 | 26[1] |
| Establishment recommendation and higher-level decision | 47 | 12 | 14 |
| Higher-level decision | 18 | 80 | 55 |
| Not answered | 1 | * | 4 |

Base: establishments with recognised trade unions covering manual workers

| | | | |
| --- | --- | --- | --- |
| *Unweighted* | *240* | *321* | *169* |
| *Weighted* | *76* | *175* | *129* |

1. See Note C.

In Tables 2.7 and 2.8 we show how prospective decisions on derecognition are related to the current structure of bargaining for manual and non-manual workers respectively. By the current structure of bargaining we mean the level at which pay was negotiated for the largest negotiating group covering that type of employee. In most cases the bargaining group was a single trade union. In a few cases bargaining occurred at more than one level and in these cases we have taken what managers considered to be the most important level in terms of the size of the increase in basic pay.

The strong association between decision-making levels on union derecognition and current bargaining levels is readily apparent in the two tables. In only 8 per cent of cases where there was enterprise level bargaining for manual workers did establishment managers say that a decision on derecognition could be taken at that level. The great majority, 80 per cent, said that it could be decided only at a higher level, normally head office. Even where bargaining currently took place at establishment level, only a third of managers said that was where any decision about derecognition would be taken; most of them would have to have any such recommendation approved by higher-level management or the matter would be purely one for corporate management. The pattern in relation to non-manual workers was very similar.

**Table 2.8**  Level of management decision-making regarding trade union derecognition at the workplace in relation to current level of bargaining for largest non-manual negotiating group, 1990

*Column percentages*

| | Most important bargaining level: | | |
| | Establishment | Enterprise | Multi-employer |
|---|---|---|---|
| **Level of decision on derecognition** | | | |
| Establishment decision | 40 | 6[1] | 15 |
| Establishment recommendation and higher-level decision | 37 | 3 | 9 |
| Higher level decision | 19 | 91 | 70 |
| Not answered | 4 | 1 | 6 |

Base: establishments with recognised trade unions covering non-manual workers

| | | | |
|---|---|---|---|
| *Unweighted* | *179* | *364* | *122* |
| *Weighted* | *40* | *233* | *86* |

1. See Note C.

Similar findings were evident when we looked at cases where unions were not currently recognised and our question about decision-making levels referred to the prospect of new recognition (Tables 2.9 and 2.10). In only 12 per cent of cases where manual workers' pay was decided on a company or enterprise-wide basis did managers say that a decision to recognise a trade union could be made at establishment level. The great majority said it would be made by corporate management or a local recommendation would need corporate approval. The pattern in relation to non-manual workers was almost identical.

This reinforces our earlier evidence, taken from the question about how recognition had come about, that trade union recognition is moderately extensive in younger workplaces, largely because of managerial considerations that lie beyond the workplace. This conclusion applies, of course, only to workplaces belonging to larger organisations – the clear majority in our sample. In single-site firms the issue is a domestic one and the extent of recognition among the younger generation of these is still substantial, at close to 30 per cent (see Table 2.5 above). Thus, even when unencumbered by wider considerations of corporate policy, managements in over a quarter of single-site firms opt for union recognition.

It is clear, then, that the extent of union recognition among younger workplaces as a whole is much lower than among older workplaces.

**Table 2.9** **Level of management decision-making regarding trade union recognition at the workplace in relation to current level of pay determination for manual workers, 1990**

*Column percentages*

| | Where pay decided on last occasion: | |
| | Establishment | Higher level |
| --- | --- | --- |
| **Level of decision on recognition** | | |
| Establishment decision | 51 | 12[1] |
| Establishment recommendation and higher-level decision | 10 | 16 |
| Higher level decision | 29 | 63 |
| Not answered | 10 | 8 |
| Base: establishments with no recognised unions covering manual workers | | |
| *Unweighted* | *224* | *144* |
| *Weighted* | *252* | *204* |

1. See Note C.

Furthermore, if this difference persisted a substantial and continuing decline in the overall extent of union recognition could be expected in the future. Indeed, it is hard to see how union recognition was ever as extensive as it was if the incidence of recognition among younger workplaces was always so much lower. The answer is that it was not.

In Table 2.11 we use data from both the 1990 and the 1980 WIRS surveys on recognition and the age of establishments to show that the age effect became much more pronounced in the 1980s. In 1980 the incidence of recognition among establishments less than ten years old was 45 per cent. In 1990 the corresponding figure was 24 per cent. The 1990 figures thus show a much lower rate of new recognition in the 1980s than must have occurred in earlier decades. When we analysed this difference across industries it appeared that the drop in the rate of recognition among newer workplaces was particularly marked within manufacturing industry. In fact, it is not putting it too strongly to say that union recognition was the norm among manufacturing plants created in the 1970s, whereas plants created in the 1980s were no more likely to recognise unions than service sector establishments, whose rate of recognition has always been much lower. Among both manufacturing and service sector establishments created in the 1980s only a quarter recognised unions.

Seen from this angle the much lower rate of creation of manufacturing plants compared with service sector establishments had no impact on the

**Table 2.10 Level of management decision-making regarding trade union recognition at the workplace in relation to current level of pay determination for non-manual workers, 1990**

*Column percentages*

| | Where pay decided on last occasion: | |
| | Establishment | Higher level |
|---|---|---|
| **Level of decision on recognition** | | |
| Establishment decision | 52 | 11[1] |
| Establishment recommendation and higher-level decision | 12 | 19 |
| Higher level decision | 28 | 64 |
| Not answered | 8 | 5 |

Base: establishments with no recognised unions covering non-manual workers

| | | |
|---|---|---|
| *Unweighted* | *354* | *244* |
| *Weighted* | *385* | *312* |

1. See Note C.

changing pattern of union recognition. It would have done so only if the historically high extent of recognition within manufacturing had been maintained among newer plants.

There can be little doubt that the lower rate of recognition among newer ⚡ workplaces in the 1980s, compared with the previous decade, arose from a widespread, general cause. The removal of the statutory support for recognition in 1980 and the decline in the presumption by managements and the state in favour of collective bargaining between trade unions and employers must surely be prime candidates. Clearly the change and its causes have important implications for the future of the trade unions and for public policy regarding them, matters to which we will return in our final chapter.

A further factor hastening the decline of union recognition is the higher ⚡ rate of turnover among establishments in the 1980s than in earlier times. In our 1990 survey 31 per cent of establishments were less than ten years old. In the 1980 survey the figure was only 19 per cent. Thus the rate of creation of new establishments (including movers) was much greater in the 1980s than in the 1970s and, given the widespread tendency for new workplaces not to recognise unions, added to the rate of decline in the extent of recognition.

**Table 2.11 Extent of union recognition by age of establishment, 1980 and 1990**

*Percentages*

| | All trading sector | Age of establishment (years) | | |
|---|---|---|---|---|
| | | 25 or more | 10-24 | Less than 10 |
| **1980 survey** | | | | |
| Proportion of establishments with any recognised union | 52 | 56 | 49 | 45 |
| Base: trading sector establishments in 1980 | | | | |
| *Unweighted base* | *1464* | *841* | *375* | *211* |
| *Weighted base* | *1432* | *745* | *371* | *266* |
| **1990 survey** | | | | |
| Proportion of establishments with any recognised union | 40 | 55[1] | 32 | 24 |
| Base: trading sector establishments in 1990 | | | | |
| *Unweighted base* | *1510* | *868* | *289* | *353* |
| *Weighted base* | *1452[2]* | *678* | *318* | *455* |

1.  Base is establishments aged 21 or more years, not 25 or more.
2.  See Note H.

## Union representation without pay bargaining rights

In our discussion so far we have adhered rigidly to a strong definition of trade union recognition that hinged upon management's recognition of the union or unions for negotiating pay. That is full recognition in the widely accepted sense. We turn now to examine whether the decline in full recognition among establishments during the 1980s, and particularly the period 1984 to 1990, was accompanied by a similar decline in weaker forms of representation that we might refer to as 'partial recognition'. In essence, was the decline in full recognition a withdrawal by management of the unions' privilege of negotiating over pay while maintaining the other elements of the unions' representational role? Or were all forms of representation by the unions at the workplace in decline?

'Partial recognition' could be defined in a number of ways. There are situations where trade unions have consultation or even negotiating rights over, for example, some conditions of employment or working practices

**Table 2.12 Degrees of union presence by various establishment characteristics, 1984 and 1990**

*Row percentages*

| | Full recog- nition | Partial recog- nition | Members but no re- cognition | No members | Un- weighted base | Weighted base |
|---|---|---|---|---|---|---|
| **1984** | | | | | | |
| All establishments | 52[1] | 1 | 9 | 39 | *1464* | *1432* |
| **1990** | | | | | | |
| All establishments | 40 | 2 | 9 | 49 | *1510* | *1452* |
| Younger establishments[2] | 27 | 3 | 8 | 63 | *267* | *316* |
| Original new work- places established 1984 onwards[2] | 29 | 1 | 12 | 59 | *74* | *91* |
| Original new work- places established 1987 onwards[3] | 32 | 5 | 15 | 54 | *41* | *41* |
| Movers[2] | 26 | 4 | 7 | 64 | *193* | *225* |
| Independent establishment | 21 | 3 | 16 | 61 | *239* | *412* |
| Part of larger organisation | 48 | 2 | 7 | 45 | *1271* | *1040* |
| Union membership density | | | | | | |
| Less than 25 per cent | 7 | 3 | 9 | 82 | *632* | *869* |
| 25 per cent or more | 100 | - | - | - | *878* | *583* |

Bases: trading sector establishments specified in row headings.

1. See Note C.
2. Source: 1990 WIRS main sample.
3. Source: Supplementary sample of new workplaces, 1990-91.

when they do not have negotiating rights over pay. These are unusual cases. More commonly, unions may have the right to represent their members in disputes or grievances with their employer while having no negotiating rights over pay.[9] It is along these lines that we have chosen to define 'partial recognition' for the purposes of the present analysis. We did briefly look at other possible definitions using, for example, the occurrence of trade union representation on consultative committees in the absence of union recognition, but these cases were so rare that such a definition would not have been illuminating. The definition we settled on was *the existence of a written procedure for dealing with disputes over discipline or dismissal that was agreed between management and trade unions (or staff associations)* in establishments without full union recognition. We assumed that if such a procedure was agreed with trade unions then managements recognised the unions for the purpose of representing employees when cases arose under the procedure. Using this definition of partial recognition gave us the results presented in Table 2.12. A number of inferences can be drawn from this.

First of all, partial recognition was never a widespread phenomenon in the recent past. In 1984 only 1 per cent of trading sector workplaces had partial recognition. In 1990 this the figure was 2 per cent. While this could be seen as an increase, it is too small to be statistically significant. The more important point is that the very substantial decline in the extent of full recognition, from 52 to 40 per cent of workplaces, was not counterbalanced by a similarly substantial rise in partial recognition. In overall terms, the change was not one from full recognition to weaker forms of recognition; it was from full recognition to no recognition.

Secondly, younger workplaces were slightly more likely to have partial recognition than older workplaces. But this tendency was confined to establishments that had moved since 1984, the move possibly providing an opportunity for management to withdraw bargaining rights. However, original new workplaces were no more likely to have partial recognition than the sample as a whole. Only 1 per cent of original new workplaces in our main sample had partial recognition; 5 per cent of original new workplaces in our small supplementary sample did so. A broad judgment would be that newly established workplaces were little different from others in this respect. Such workplaces were distinctive in their lower rate of full recognition and their greater likelihood of having trade union members but no form of recognition by management. This, combined with the fact that it was single independent workplaces (small firms) that were most likely to have union members present but no form of recognition for representation or negotiating purposes, suggests again that it was unfavourable management attitudes to union activity that were partly responsible.

Thirdly, there was clearly an association between partial recognition and low levels of membership. In fact, none of the cases of partial recognition were ones where union members accounted for more than a quarter of the workforce. By contrast, in most cases where unions had full recognition, membership levels were well above this level.

A final piece of evidence about union representation in the absence of full recognition comes from our panel sample. Did establishments that had derecognised trade unions between 1984 and 1990 (some 9 per cent of our panel sample) have partial recognition in 1990? Using the definition of partial recognition given above, the answer is that only a minority of 13 per cent did so. Our base for this estimate is relatively small, but it gives a clear indication that where managements withdrew trade union recognition they generally did so on a comprehensive basis. Only a few continued to allow the union or unions a limited, representative role.

The broad conclusion, then, is that the decline in union representation between 1984 and 1990 was not generally a weakening of the role of unions from one of full negotiation and representation to a partial role involving only representational rights in individual grievances or disciplinary disputes. Rather, it involved a wholesale reduction of the role of trade unions. Some of this occurred through derecognition, but the more substantial part of it arose because the unions were unable to replace the unionised workplaces that closed down with similar numbers of newer workplaces where they established full recognition. It is not oversimplifying the picture to say that the decline in union recognition was accompanied by a corresponding rise in complete non-unionism.

**Notes and references**

1. Neil Millward and Mark Stevens, *British Workplace Industrial Relations 1980-1984,* Gower, Aldershot, 1986.

2. The associations mentioned here are largely in conformity with those reported from econometric work in D.G. Blanchflower and A.J. Oswald, 'The Determinants of Plant Closures', Dartmouth College mimeo, 1989. That work looked at census units which were part of (or the whole of) establishments that had closed down between the 1981 Census of Employment and the 1984 WIRS. The data from census units was limited to a handful of variables and Blanchflower and Oswald therefore used industry-based proxies for union presence and other important variables. The data from the 1984-1990 panel, used here, are far more satisfactory and, to our knowledge, are a unique source of statistical information on plant closures.

3. We use the term *aggregate union density* here, as in our earlier volume, to refer to the total of union members (where known) in the sample divided by the total number of employees in those workplaces. It is not the proportion in each workplace averaged across the sample.

4. R. Butchart, 'A new UK definition of the high technology industries', *Economic Trends,* No.400, February 1987, pp.82-88.

5. A detailed econometric analysis of union recognition in the three WIRS surveys was recently reported by Richard Disney, Stephen Machin and Amanda Gosling, 'What Has Happened to Union Recognition in Britain?', Centre for Economic

Performance, London School of Economics, Discussion Paper No.130, 1993. It concluded that the probability of recognition in new plants was much lower in the 1980s than in earlier time periods.

6.  Results from our supplementary sample of new workplaces pointed in the same direction as all the main sample results presented in this paragraph, but the number of cases is too small to give any weight to them.

7.  Separate codes were used for UK and overseas head offices, but these have been combined in the results presented here.

8.  A postal survey of 457 multi-plant companies in the late 1980s using the Exstat database reported that in 44 per cent of them no establishments had recognised unions, in 22 per cent all establishments had recognised unions, while in 35 per cent of them some establishments did and others did not. See Paul Gregg and Anthony Yates, 'Changes in wage-setting arrangements and trade union presence in the 1980s', *British Journal of Industrial Relations,* vol.29, no.3, September 1991, pp.361-76.

9.  The converse type of case – where unions have negotiating rights over pay but not the right to represent members in, for example, individual greivances or disciplinay matters – must be extremely rare. In only 5 per cent of workplaces with a recognised union did managers say that the disciplinary procedure was not formally agreed with the union or staff association.

# 3 Single union representation

'Single union deals' were one of the prime ingredients of the 'new industrial relations' of the late 1980s. They attracted much attention and controversy, mostly concerning the agreements to limit strike activity and to allow management complete freedom in the organisation of work. Rather less attention was given to the general arguments for and against the representation of workers by a single trade union. It was the identity and policies of the particular trade unions most actively involved in pursuing single union deals that aroused the most controversy, especially within the trade union movement. The arrangements were branded by their trade union detractors as 'sweetheart deals', the result of managements choosing the most compliant union in exchange for granting sole representation rights.

Although the pace of introduction of single union deals appears to have slackened since the late 1980s,[1] the issue of single union representation has by no means sunk into oblivion. It remains a topical issue for two important reasons. Firstly, single union representation is of interest because of the new legislation recently enacted by Parliament. The Trade Union Reform and Employment Rights Act includes measures to give individual employees greater freedom to join the union of their choice.[2] Such choices will be able to be made by employees irrespective of any understandings between trade unions about which occupations, industries or sectors of employment they prefer to recruit in and possibly with little regard to the existing structure of representation at workplace, employer and industry level. The new legislation could encourage a proliferation of unrecognised unions within some workplaces. And it could lead to the undermining of single union agreements by facilitating the recruitment of employees by rival unions which might then claim recognition from employers with such agreements.

The second reason for being interested in single union representation is the long-standing debate in the field of industrial relations about the pros and cons of single and multi-union representation, particularly with regard to collective bargaining. Before the advent of the WIRS series this debate had little basis in systematically collected research data, but it was widely believed that multi-unionism was economically detrimental, in terms of

35

increased dispute activity and higher management costs, both for settling pay increases and for introducing change of various kinds. A recent analysis of the 1984 WIRS has put the debate on a better empirical footing.[3] It concludes that it was not multi-unionism *per se* that produced undesirable economic effects but the presence of multiple bargaining units in workplaces with multiple recognised unions.

Against this background, and to set the scene for our examination of single union agreements, it seems pertinent to use the WIRS material to give an overview of single union representation. The question behind this is what leads a workplace to have a single trade union representing employees rather that several unions representing them. In addition, which sectors and industries most commonly have single union representation? Is it largely confined to the few unions that were most active in the 1980s in pursuing single union agreements? Is it a special feature of younger workplaces? What types of representation does it involve? In examining these questions we confine our attention for most of this chapter to workplaces with trade union members. We begin by examining our broadest indicator of possible employee representation by trade unions, the presence of union members at the workplace.

### Single and multi-union workplaces – union presence

It may be something of a surprise that it is more common for workplaces in British industry and commerce with union members to have a single trade union present than multiple unions. Of all workplaces in industry and commerce, the presence of union members, as reported by our management respondents, was as follows:

- 49 per cent had no union members
- 27 per cent had members of a single union
- 23 per cent had members of two or more unions.

Among workplaces with union members, the base for the ensuing discussion, 54 per cent had members of a single union. As we have shown in our earlier volumes on the WIRS series, multi-unionism is more common in larger establishments and single unionism correspondingly declines as establishment size increases. The pattern with respect to size was particularly clear from the fact that the average size of a single union workplace was 84 employees, whereas for multi-union workplaces it was 165. However, the relationship between workplace size and the tendency to have single rather than multi-union representation was not a smooth one. There seemed to be a particularly sharp change at around 500 employees; above this size the proportion of workplaces with members of a single union dropped to well below 20 per cent.

The overall inverse relationship between establishment size and the presence of a single union meant that fewer employees worked in single-union workplaces compared with the proportion of workplaces with a single union. The proportion of employees in workplaces with members of a single trade union was 37 per cent. Thus only a minority of employees in workplaces with union members present are employed in single-union situations.

Naturally, a number of factors lie behind the complexity of union presence at individual workplaces. These will include the historical development of trade unionism in the industry, including the history of union amalgamations (and much less frequent breakaways) and whether the workplace employs a wide range of occupations and, particularly, skilled workers with a craft-based tradition. Other situations will be explicable more in terms of employers' attitudes to multi-unionism or to particular trade unions. Whatever the historical explanations, the picture in 1990 given by WIRS is of a wide variation across industries and types of workplace in the extent to which union members at a workplace were concentrated within a single union.

Besides their size, mentioned above, six characteristics of workplaces predisposed them towards the presence of a single union rather than multiple unions. First, membership of a single union was more common in the private sector than in public sector workplaces; indeed, 100 per cent of the publicly-owned trading sector establishments in our 1990 sample were multi-union.[4] Second, head offices (with their high proportion of non-manual staff) more often had single unions; 63 per cent of our sample of head offices with union members did so, compared with 54 per cent of all workplaces with members. Thirdly, workplaces with a high proportion of part-time employees tended to have a single union. Fourthly, workplaces in the services sector more commonly had a single union; 61 per cent did so compared with 50 per cent in manufacturing.[5] Fifthly, younger workplaces tended to have single unionism. Sixthly, single union presence at workplace level was a feature of particular industries, much but not all of this because some unions are industry specific in their recruitment policies. These last two features merit some elaboration.

The tendency for younger workplaces to have members of single rather than multiple unions was, perhaps surprisingly, not confined to those workplaces that had come into existence in the 1980s, when single union arrangements came into the public eye. The tendency predated 1980 by at least ten years. On the basis of our 1990 survey evidence, establishments created in the 1970s (and still in existence in 1990) had the highest proportion of single unionism; 69 per cent of them did so compared with

66 per cent of more recent workplaces. It was only among those created before 1970 that the proportion, at 44 per cent, was substantially lower.[6] Single union representation is by no means a recent development in British industrial relations.

Furthermore, none of the tendency for workplaces established since the 1970s to have single rather than multi-union representation was explicable in terms of differences in size. When we controlled for size of workplace in our analysis, the differences were just as apparent. Of course, it can be plausibly argued that the current size of a workplace is not the most relevant measure of size in this matter; it may be that its current complexity of union representation is more a reflection of its size and occupational structure at some point in the past. Without historical data on both size and representation structure in our datasets it is impossible to address this argument satisfactorily. However, the retrospective data on size that we do have, measuring size six years previously, can be used to answer it in a partial way. When we did this analysis it suggested that multi-union workplaces established before 1970 were no more likely to have contracted in size between 1984 and 1990 than single union workplaces of comparable age. Admittedly, this is not an adequate test. But it points to factors in addition to size as being important in explaining the current proportions of multi-union and single union workplaces.

Table 3.1 gives a more detailed analysis of the extent of single unionism among our categories of younger workplaces. In the group as a whole (those up to six years old) 64 per cent of workplaces with union members had just a single union present, compared with 52 per cent for older workplaces. Among younger workplaces, recent movers and original new workplaces in our main sample had exactly the same proportions of single union representation. Only in our supplementary sample of new workplaces was there a suggestion of single union representation being more common.

From the lower half of Table 3.1 it appears that the tendency for younger workplaces to have a single union was confined to the service sector of the economy. Among older workplaces the proportion having a single union was 51 per cent in manufacturing and 52 per cent in the service sector. However, among younger workplaces the figures were 42 per cent for manufacturing and 75 per cent for services. The low figure for manufacturing may be something of a surprise, but it is explained by the fact that the great majority of younger manufacturing workplaces were movers and these were much more likely to be multi-union. The very small numbers of original new manufacturing plants that had union members were more likely to be single-union, but they formed a small part of the overall picture. It was largely the higher incidence of single unionism

**Table 3.1  Proportion of workplaces with union members having a single union, 1990**

*Percentages*

|  |  | Unweighted base | Weighted base |
|---|---|---|---|
| All workplaces | 54 | *1021* | *739* |
| Older workplaces | 52 | *898* | *621* |
| Younger workplaces[1] | 64 | *123* | *118* |
| Original new workplaces established 1984 onwards[1] | (64) | *39* | *37* |
| Original new workplaces established 1987 onwards[2] | (74) | *19* | *19* |
| Movers[1] | 64 | *84* | *81* |
| **Manufacturing** |  |  |  |
| Older workplaces | 51 | *455* | *207[3]* |
| Younger workplaces | (42) | *43* | *39* |
| **Services** |  |  |  |
| Older workplaces | 52 | *443* | *413* |
| Younger workplaces | 75 | *80* | *80* |

Base: trading sector establishments with union members

1. Source: 1990 WIRS main sample.
2. Source: supplementary sample of new workplaces, 1990-91.
3. See Note H.

among younger workplaces in the service industries that accounted for the difference between younger and older workplaces in the trading sector as a whole.

It is well known, and clearly confirmed in all the WIRS surveys, that union membership and other measures of trade union strength are generally lower in private services than in manufacturing industry. Because of this it seems natural to ask whether the greater propensity for younger service sector establishments to have a single union is in some respects a manifestation of weaker union representation. We shall address this question later in the chapter when we examine various characteristics of union representation in single union workplaces. Before doing this we look further at the picture of single union representation in terms of industries and the types of union involved.

*The industries and unions involved in single-union presence*
Table 3.2 gives, for 21 separate industrial sectors, two measures of union presence in trading sector workplaces: the presence of a single union, where

there are members present; and (for contextual purposes) the presence of any union members among all establishments in the sector. Some of the sectors with a high incidence of single union presence are ones where a relatively low proportion of workplaces have any union members present. Wholesale and retail distribution and the clothing and footwear industry fit this pattern. Other industries, for example, banking and finance, transport, metal manufacture, textiles and construction have relatively high numbers of workplaces with a single union, but also have high union presence overall. Some of these have industry specific unions. At the other extreme, there are three industrial sectors that have very few single-union workplaces: posts and telecommunications; energy and water supply; and hotels and catering. The first two of these (both dominated by ex-public sector employers) have very high union presence, with over 95 per cent of workplaces having members among the workforce. The third sector, hotels and catering, has very few workplaces with members, but of those that do a majority have a single union. Broadly speaking there is no clear relationship between an industry's tendency to have single union representation and the extent of union presence in the industry.

The pattern across industrial sectors of single union representation varied partly according to the existence of industry-specific unions. Examples of this included USDAW in retailing, UCATT in construction and BIFU in the banking and finance sector. But neither UCATT nor BIFU had a clear monopoly of single union representation in those industries; their competitors included EETPU and MSF respectively.

A second feature of the pattern was the degree to which the general unions, TGWU and GMB, were spread across sectors and apparently competed within sectors. Thus within the 11 manufacturing sectors distinguished in our analysis, three had only TGWU cases of single union representation, three had only GMB cases and five sectors had both TGWU and GMB cases in the same sector. There was no sector within manufacturing where neither of these two general unions did not have some cases of single union representation.

In service industries the spread of the two big general unions was more limited. Of the nine sectors distinguished, one had just TGWU cases of single union representation, five had both TGWU and GMB cases and one had just GMB cases. The remaining three sectors had no cases where the general unions had single union representation; in these sectors industry-specific unions either predominated or competed with smaller general unions like MSF.

Further detail of the characteristics of unions in relation to single union representation is given in Table 3.3. The first column shows the extent to

**Table 3.2  Proportion of workplaces in industry and commerce with any union members and with a single union with members, 1990**

*Percentages*

| | Any union member | A single union |
|---|---|---|
| All industry and commerce | 51 | 27 |
| All manufacturing | 58 | 29 |
| Metals and mineral products (21-24)[1] | 77 | 51 |
| Chemicals and manufactured fibres (25-26) | 66 | 26 |
| Metal goods (31) | 61 | 29 |
| Mechanical engineering (32) | 73 | 27 |
| Electrical and instrument engineering (33-34, 37) | 40 | 22 |
| Vehicles and transport equipment (35-36) | 52 | 24 |
| Food, drink and tobacco (41-42) | 51 | 17 |
| Textiles (43) | 76 | 45 |
| Leather, footwear and clothing (44-45) | 43 | 33 |
| Timber and furniture, paper and printing (46-47) | 63 | 28 |
| Rubber, plastics and other manufacturing (48-49) | 32 | 23 |
| All services | 48 | 27 |
| Energy and water (11-17) | 96 | 6 |
| Construction (50) | 57 | 46 |
| Wholesale distribution (61-63) | 40 | 31 |
| Retail distribution (64-65) | 46 | 40 |
| Hotels, catering, repairs (66-67) | 13 | 9 |
| Transport (71-77) | 75 | 35 |
| Posts and telecommunications (79) | 99 | 1 |
| Banking, finance, insurance (81-82) | 88 | 47 |
| Business services (83-85) | 16 | 15 |
| Other services (92, 94, 96-99) | 47 | 28 |

Bases:  first column - establishments in industry and commerce
second column - establishments with union members present

1.  Industry codes in brackets from the *Standard Industrial Classification 1980*

which the ten unions most frequently having members within workplaces in the WIRS sample were the only union with members present. Together these ten unions accounted for nearly 80 per cent of all cases with a single union present. Britain's largest union in terms of membership, the TGWU, accounted for nearly a quarter of all such cases. The union most prominent in the negotiation of 'single union deals' in the 1980s, the EETPU,[7] was responsible for just 6 per cent of cases.

**Table 3.3** **Characteristics of the ten unions most commonly involved in single union representation at workplace level, 1990**

*Percentages*

|  | Workplaces where named union was only union with members as a proportion of all workplaces with members of a single union | Workplaces where named union was only union as a proportion of all workplaces where it had members | Number of industrial sectors (out of 19) in which union had sole representation in any workplace |
|---|---|---|---|
| TGWU | 23 | 46 | 14 |
| USDAW | 12 | 77 | 3 |
| GMB | 9 | 30 | 14 |
| AEU | 7 | 25 | 8 |
| EETPU | 6 | 27 | 7 |
| BIFU | 6 | 35 | 1 |
| UCATT | 5 | 51 | 2 |
| NGA | 4 | 43 | 2 |
| SOGAT | 3 | 37 | 4 |
| MSF | 3 | 19 | 6 |

Bases: as specified in column headings

The second column in the table shows what proportion of all workplaces in which it has members is accounted for by cases where it is the only union with members present. This can be thought of as the union's propensity towards exclusive representation at workplace level. On this measure USDAW is most involved in single union representation. At the other end of the spectrum, AEU, EETPU and MSF are rarely the only union in the workplaces where they have members. Given the prominence of EETPU and AEU in reported single-union deals, their lack of prominence among cases of single union representation is noteworthy.

In the third column of Table 3.3 we show the range of industries in which the ten unions have any cases of single representation. Out of the 19 industries[8] in which there were substantial numbers of workplaces having a single union, the two large general unions TGWU and GMB occurred at least once in 14 of them. Among the others, AEU, EETPU and MSF were present on a single-union basis in well under half of the 19 sectors. BIFU, UCATT and the NGA were most clearly industry-specific unions.

From this we can see that single union representation is widely spread amongst unions and industries. Only one union, USDAW, comes close to being an industry-specific union that has no other unions present at workplaces where it has members. And in the industry in which it is concentrated, retailing, it is by no means the only union with members; other workplaces in retailing have members of other unions, mostly commonly the TGWU. The pattern of membership among union members in British workplaces is a very long way from the tidy pattern of industrial unionism that some countries have.

## The nature of single union representation

We now turn to examine some of the main characteristics of union representation in workplaces with a single union. We compare them with multi-union workplaces on the basis of membership density, recognition, coverage and so on to see whether there is something distinctive about single union representation.

### *Membership density and type of employee*

It should cause little surprise that trade union membership density was substantially lower in workplaces with a single union than in those with multiple unions. Our earlier analysis showed that single union representation was more common in smaller workplaces, in the service sector, where part-time employees were more prevalent, and so on; all of these factors are associated with lower levels of trade union membership. But the size of the difference may be something of a surprise. In overall terms, 46 per cent of employees were union members where there was a single union, compared with 72 per cent where there were multiple unions.

Table 3.4 shows how union membership density is distributed within single union and multi-union workplaces. The whole distribution for single union workplaces inclines towards the lower end, whereas for multi-union workplaces it inclines towards the upper end. Three times as many single union workplaces have membership density below a quarter as multi-union workplaces do. At the top end of the distribution two and a half times as many multi-union workplaces have membership density of 90 per cent or more than is the case for single union workplaces.

When we controlled for a number of the factors predisposing workplaces towards single union rather than multi-union representation the lower levels of membership in single union workplaces remained very substantial. Notably, controlling for size of workplace and, separately, for the proportion of the workforce employed part-time had little impact on the differences. Two factors that did help explain the lower levels of membership density of single union workplaces were the types of employee in membership and the lack of recognition of the union by management. We deal with each of these in turn.

**Table 3.4   The distribution of union membership density within single union and multi-union workplaces, 1990**

|  | Number of unions with members | |
|  | 1 | 2 or more |
| --- | --- | --- |
|  |  | *Column percentages* |
| **Proportion of workplaces with union density of:** |  |  |
| 1-24% | 32[1] | 10 |
| 25-49% | 16 | 11 |
| 50-74% | 23 | 26 |
| 75-89% | 8 | 20 |
| 90-99% | 7 | 14 |
| 100% | 3 | 10 |
| Not answered | 10 | 10 |
|  |  | *Means* |
| Overall mean density (per cent) | 46 | 72 |
| Base: trading sector establishments with union members | | |
| *Unweighted* | *337* | *684* |
| *Weighted* | *399* | *340* |

1.   See Note C.

From our questions about which unions had members at the workplace and which types of employee were members of them we were able to measure how segregated workplaces were with respect to union membership. Our questions recorded whether each union with members at a sampled workplace had members: only among the manual workforce; only among the non-manual workforce; among both manual and non-manual employees. In looking at the degree of segregation of union recruitment we confine our attention to workplaces with both manual and non-manual employees (about 90 per cent of workplaces with union members). The broad picture that emerges is of a high degree of segregation in union membership. Nearly a half of workplaces with union members (and with both manual and non-manual employees) had members from among only one section of the workforce, but not from both.

As the first column in Table 3.5 shows, the most common type of segregated membership was for a workplace to have only manual workers in membership. This was so for 41 per cent of workplaces. In a mere 5 per cent of workplaces all union members were white-collar employees. The majority of workplaces (53 per cent) had a mixture of manual and white-collar union members. However, membership segregation was substantially higher in single union workplaces. Nearly 70 per cent of single union workplaces had segregated membership and nearly all of these had only manual members (Table 3.5). By contrast, only around 20 per cent of multi-union workplaces had segregated membership. Multi-unionism appears to increase greatly the likelihood of a broader range of occupations being represented by trade unions. This should not be taken as implying that multi-unionism causes the broader spread of employees to have union representation. In some circumstances it might be the opposite, groups excluded from current arrangements joining another union and then seeking representational rights. At this stage our statement is merely a descriptive one, that in workplaces with multiple unions a broader range of occupational groups had union representation.

However, in single union workplaces the spread of membership does appear to be have been limited by the traditional recruitment pattern of the union that was present. Some trade unions clearly attracted members only from among the manual workers at workplaces where they were the sole union present. The most striking cases of this were the AEU and UCATT. Our sample contained virtually no cases where these unions were the only union with members and had any non-manual members. The large general unions, TGWU and GMB, had only manual members in the clear majority of cases where they were the only union. So did the EETPU. In contrast, USDAW and BIFU had both manual and non-manual members in the great majority of cases where they were the only union. MSF was the only one among the 12 unions identified in this analysis which most frequently represented only white-collar employees.

The lower levels of membership density in single union workplaces appear, then, to be partly explicable in terms of the inability of unions to appeal to employees outside the occupations that have traditionally formed their membership base. In single union workplaces with a predominantly manual trade union, white-collar employees may see little attraction in being represented by such a union. Indeed, we found from our separate questioning on this matter that unsuccessful attempts to recruit white-collar workers into union membership were quite common in workplaces where only manual workers were union members; around a fifth of such workplaces had experienced recruitment attempts in the six years prior to our survey. As we mentioned in our earlier volume, such circumstances were associated with negative attitudes towards unions on the part of

**Table 3.5  Types of employee in union membership within single union and multi-union workplaces, 1990**

*Column percentages*

| | All workplaces | Number of unions with members 1 | 2 or more |
|---|---|---|---|
| **Proportion of workplaces with union members among:** | | | |
| Only the manual workforce | 41[1] | 63 | 17 |
| Only the non-manual workforce | 5 | 5 | 5 |
| Both manual and non-manual employees | 53 | 32 | 78 |

Base: trading sector establishments with both manual and non-manual employees and with some union members

| | | | |
|---|---|---|---|
| *Unweighted* | *940* | *300* | *640* |
| *Weighted* | *635* | *341* | *294* |

1.See Note C.

management. The converse type of case, where predominantly white-collar unions had failed to recruit manual workers into membership, was much less common and appeared more a matter of the union not attempting to recruit small groups of workers.

Union membership levels are not wholly, or perhaps even largely, explainable by the nature of individual trade unions, their recruitment practices and employees' perceptions of the unions. Managements' willingness to recognise trade unions is a key factor in membership levels. Is it lack of recognition that explains much of the lower level of membership in single union workplaces? We address this question after examining the basic differences in the extent of union recognition between single union and multi-union workplaces.

*Union recognition*
In chapter 2 we used two definitions of the recognition of trade unions by management. We used the term *full recognition* to describe situations where management recognised the trade union or unions for negotiating levels of pay. We used the term *partial recognition* to describe situations where there was not full recognition but where there was a written procedure for dealing with disputes over discipline or dismissal and that procedure was agreed between management and unions. These are key

**Table 3.6  Extent of union recognition among single union and multi-union workplaces, 1990**

*Column percentages*

| | Number of unions with members | |
| --- | --- | --- |
| | 1 | 2 or more |
| **Proportion of workplaces with:** | | |
| Union members, but no recognition | 23 | 12 |
| Partial recognition | 4 | 2 |
| Full recognition | 73 | 86[1] |
| Base:  trading sector establishments with union members | | |
| *Unweighted* | *337* | *684* |
| *Weighted* | *399* | *340* |

1.  Full recognition for at least one union.

indicators of the role of unions at workplace level. Table 3.6 shows how single and multi-union workplaces differ on these key indicators.

In terms of full recognition, unions were substantially less likely to have achieved this status if they were the only union at the workplace. Full recognition existed in 73 per cent of workplaces with a single union, compared with 86 per cent of workplaces with several unions present. Moreover, the deficit in single union workplaces with respect to full recognition was not made up by a correspondingly higher rate of partial recognition. They were more likely to have partial recognition – 4 per cent did so compared with 2 per cent of multi-union workplaces. But the main difference was that single union workplaces were much more likely (indeed, twice as likely) to have no form of recognition by management at all. To a substantial degree, therefore, single unionism is a weaker form of trade union representation in overall terms than multi-unionism, based upon the ability of the unions concerned to achieve full or partial recognition by management.

Taking full recognition as the prime indicator of trade union represent-ation, the overall picture within industry and commerce in 1990 is shown in Table 3.7, separating cases with single and multiple recognised unions. Taking all workplaces (whether they contained union members or not) 22 per cent had a single recognised union, 18 per cent had two or more recognised unions and the remaining 60 per cent had no recognised unions. Taking only workplaces with union members, the proportion with a single

**Table 3.7 Proportion of workplaces with different numbers of recognised unions, 1990**

*Column percentages*

|  | All establishments | Establishments with union members | Establishments with any recognised unions |
|---|---|---|---|
| **Number of recognised unions:** | | | |
| None | 60 | 21 | - |
| One | 22 | 43 | 54 |
| Two or more | 18 | 36 | 46 |
| Base: establishments in industry and commerce as specified in column heads | | | |
| *Unweighted* | *1510* | *1021* | *903* |
| *Weighted* | *1452* | *739* | *584* |

recognised union was 43 per cent. Among workplaces with recognised unions, the proportion with a single recognised union was 54 per cent.

Single union recognition was notably associated with younger workplaces, as our earlier discussion of single union presence might have suggested. Table 3.8 gives results from our 1990 main sample and the supplementary sample of new establishments. Taking the main sample results, at first sight the tendency for younger workplaces to have single rather than multiple recognised unions is clear: 17 per cent have a single recognised union, compared with 10 per cent with multiple recognised unions. For older workplaces the proportions are nearer parity (23 per cent and 21 per cent respectively). Separating out the two types of younger workplace gives the rather surprising result that it was not original new workplaces that had the greater tendency towards recognition of a single union, rather than multiple unions. It was establishments that moved that showed this tendency: 18 per cent had a single recognised union, whereas only 8 per cent had multiple recognised unions. Movers had characteristics such as a smaller size and a predominantly white-collar workforce provided something of an explanation for this lower rate of multiple unionism. But the finding that as many new original workplaces have multiple recognised unions as have a single recognised union seems contrary to conventional wisdom. However, it should be remembered that our main survey sample excluded the very newest establishments, those set up from 1988 onwards. Our supplementary sample, albeit small, did cover those set in 1988 to 1991 and these results do show a much lower incidence of multiple unionism,

**Table 3.8** **Number of recognised unions, by age of workplace**

*Column percentages*

| | Older workplaces (pre 1984) | Younger workplaces[1] | Original new workplaces established 1984 onwards[1] | Original new workplaces established 1987 onwards[2] | Movers 1984 onwards[1] | Movers 1987 onwards[2] |
|---|---|---|---|---|---|---|
| **Number of recognised unions:** | | | | | | |
| None | 56 | 74[3] | 71 | (69) | 74 | (77) |
| One | 23 | 17 | 15 | (24) | 18 | (17) |
| Two or more | 21 | 10 | 14 | (7) | 8 | (6) |
| Base: establishments in industry and commerce | | | | | | |
| *Unweighted* | *1243* | *267* | *74* | *41* | *193* | *18* |
| *Weighted* | *1135* | *316* | *91* | *41* | *225* | *18* |

1.   Source: 1990 WIRS main sample.
2.   Source: Supplementary sample of new workplaces, 1990-91
3.   See Note C.

both among original new workplaces and among those that had moved from elsewhere since 1988. For these most recently formed workplaces single union recognition outnumbered multiple recognition by around three to one. The tendency towards single union recognition at workplace level may thus have accelerated towards the start of the current decade.

## Recent moves towards single union recognition

The extent of employee representation by a single recognised trade union, given above, stands in some contrast to the widespread characterisation of the British economy as one with a unionised sector dominated by multi-union arrangements. Of course that characterisation is fair when one is considering the institutions of national, multi-employer bargaining that still remain, which almost without exception have more than a single trade union on the employees' side. It is also generally a fair characterisation when the focus of attention is at the level of industries. And in the public services sector, excluded from the present analysis, multi-union representation is very much the norm. However, in industry and commerce that is clearly not the case.

Whether the predominance of single unionism was a recent development and, if so, how it had come about were naturally matters of interest in an investigation of recent developments in workplace industrial relations. Our 1990 survey therefore contained new questions on these matters. The questions were confined to the 40 per cent of workplaces where trade unions were recognised for collective bargaining over pay. We sought information on the number of recognised trade unions three years previously and, where there had been a change in the number, how the change had come about. From the first question it appears that about 5 per cent of workplaces with a single recognised union in 1990 had had two or more recognised unions in 1987. In virtually all of these cases the previous number of unions had been two. By far the most common reason given by managers for the change was that membership of the union that was no longer recognised had dwindled away. Other reasons given were union mergers, the disappearance of jobs covered by the union in question and the transfer of union members to the remaining union. These results contrast sharply with the reasons given for reductions in the number of unions in workplaces that remained multi-union. In these, generally much larger, workplaces the most common reason was union mergers. A further question on management attempts to change bargaining arrangements in the preceding three years indicated that such moves were rare. A move towards dealing with fewer unions was reported in 5 per cent of workplaces with recognised unions. It was in workplaces with three or more unions that such moves were concentrated, suggesting that it was the more complex types of representation that gave most cause for concern, rather than situations where just two unions were involved.

From this brief analysis it appears that very little of the extent of single union representation in 1990 could be accounted for by recent changes from multi-union to single union representation.

*Collective bargaining coverage in single-union workplaces*

From their lower levels of union membership it would be reasonable to infer that single union workplaces contained fewer workers covered by collective bargaining than would be the case in workplaces with multi-union representation. Table 3.9 gives the relevant results. In overall terms, collective bargaining in 1990 covered 43 per cent of employees in industry and commerce and 79 per cent of employees in workplaces with recognised trade unions. Amongst workplaces with a single recognised trade union it was 66 per cent, compared with 86 per cent where there were multiple recognised unions. The substantially lower coverage of collective bargaining was mirrored almost precisely by the membership density levels in the two types of workplace, the corresponding figures being 56 and 76 per cent.

Much of the difference in coverage between workplaces with single and multiple recognised unions is accounted for by the large number of single-union establishments where the union had only manual workers as members. In such cases coverage was less than half. By contrast, unions that had recruited both manual and non-manual workers into membership (at workplaces where there was a single union) represented nearly 80 per cent of employees, close to the figure for multi-union workplaces. It is clear that, judged by the yardstick of what proportion of employees is represented for bargaining purposes, single union representation is generally weaker than multi-union representation.

*Union representatives and their facilities*

Our two final indicators of the nature of trade union organisation in single union workplaces concern, first, the presence at the workplace of representatives or shop stewards and, secondly, the existence of check-off arrangements for union subscriptions. The main WIRS questions on the existence and numbers of union representatives were confined to workplaces with recognised trade unions. It is those questions that we use here, combining a number of them to classify workplaces as having or not having any representatives of recognised unions. Overall, 70 per cent of workplaces in industry and commerce with recognised trade unions had a workplace representative, the remainder relying on local union officers or

**Table 3.9** **Proportion of employees covered by collective bargaining and union membership density in single and multi-union workplaces, 1990**

*Means*

|  | Percentage of employees covered | Union membership density | *Unweighted base* | *Weighted base* |
|---|---|---|---|---|
| All trading sector | 43 | 39 | *1510* | *1452* |
| **Workplaces with:** |  |  |  |  |
| No recognised unions | - | 4 | *607* | *868* |
| Any recognised unions | 79 | 69 | *903* | *584* |
| More than one recognised union | 86 | 76 | *612*[1] | *268* |
| A single recognised union | 66 | 56 | *257* | *289* |
| **Workplaces with a single recognised union having:** |  |  |  |  |
| Manual members only | 49 | 44 | *118* | *154* |
| Non-manual members only | (78) | (55) | *39* | *64* |
| Both manual and non-manual members | 77 | 68 | *132* | *96* |

Base: all trading sector establishments

---

1. See Note G.

(more commonly) representatives from other establishments of the same employer. Table 3.10 shows how the overall figure of 70 per cent is decomposed when we separate single from multi-union workplaces. It also shows separate figures for older and younger workplaces.

Single union workplaces were less likely to have their own representatives, but the difference was not very large – 66 per cent, compared with 74 per cent for multi-union workplaces. Differences of a similar order were apparent between older workplaces (72 per cent) and younger workplaces (62 per cent). Besides younger workplaces being less likely to have their own representatives, smaller workplaces and those with lower levels of membership density were also less likely to have them. Given this, we controlled for workplace size in our analysis, and the differences between older single and multi-union workplaces became insignificant. However, among younger workplaces there was still a tendency for single union workplaces to be less likely to have their own representatives. Clear conclusions from this analysis were difficult to draw. But it did seem that,

**Table 3.10 Presence of union representatives at single and multi-union workplaces, by age of workplace, 1990**

*Percentages*

|  | Any recognised unions | Single union | Multi-union |
|---|---|---|---|
| **Proportion of workplaces having representatives** |  |  |  |
| All workplaces | 70 | 66 | 74 |
| Older workplaces | 72 | 68 | 75 |
| Younger workplaces | 62 | 56 | 69 |

Base: trading sector workplaces with recognised unions

among workplaces with recognised trade unions, the combination of characteristics least likely to give rise to the presence of an on-site trade union representative was a single recognised union in a younger workplace. Taking the absence of a representative as an indicator of weak union organisation at workplace level, single union representation appeared to be somewhat weaker in so far as it was more common in younger workplaces, rather than because it was more common in smaller workplaces.

We have used the presence of local, lay union representatives as an indicator of the strength of union organisation as it had emerged from employees themselves. However, unions generally gain in strength when they are recognised and accepted by management and our second indicator refers to this aspect of union strength. For this we use the presence of a check-off arrangement, that is, an arrangement whereby the employer deducts union subscriptions from the union members' pay and transfers the funds directly to the union (usually free of charge). The results, for workplaces with recognised unions, are summarised in Table 3.11.

In most respects the pattern of differences resembled that for the results on the presence of union representatives, outlined above. Workplaces least likely to have check-off arrangements were younger workplaces with a single recognised union; 63 per cent of them did so compared with 83 per cent for all workplaces with recognised unions. However, the age effect was more pronounced in relation to check-off. This might suggest a recent decline in employers' generally favourable view of check-off arrangements, a change which would be easier to put into effect in newer workplaces.[9] Again, any lower level of union strength in single union workplaces, using check-off as our indicator, appeared to be because more of them were younger and smaller rather than because they were single union rather than multi-union.

**Table 3.11 Existence of check-off arrangements at single and multi-union workplaces, by age of workplace, 1990**

*Percentages*

|  | Any recognised unions | Single union | Multi-union |
|---|---|---|---|
| **Proportion of workplaces having check-off arrangements** | | | |
| All workplaces | 83 | 79 | 86 |
| Older workplaces | 85 | 83 | 87 |
| Younger workplaces | 70 | 63 | 82 |

Base: trading sector workplaces with recognised unions

**Notes and references**

1. Gregor Gall, 'What happened to single union deals? – a research note', *Industrial Relations Journal,* vol.24, no.1, 1993, pp.71-75.

2. The Act allows a trade union to refuse membership to those who have no commonality of interest with its existing members, for example on the basis of their occupations or geographical location. See, 'The Trade Union Reform and Employment Rights Act 1993: a section by section guide', *Employment Gazette,* vol.101, no.8, pp.345-56.

3. S. Machin, M. Stewart and J. Van Reenen (1992), 'The Economic Effects of Multiple Unionism: Evidence from the 1984 Workplace Industrial Relations Survey', Centre for Economic Performance Discussion Paper No.66.

4. It is also true that our private sector sample in 1990 included multi-union establishments which had previously been under public ownership, but without a precise question on changes of ownership due to privatisation these cannot all be identified.

5. These figures refer to the private sector.

6. It would be desirable to confirm this from our earlier surveys, but this is not possible because in both 1980 and 1984 our questions about union presence were asked separately for manual and non-manual workers. Where both types of worker had union members it is impossible to determine reliably from our questions whether they were members of a single union.

7. Gregor Gall, op.cit.

8. Two industries, energy and water supply and posts and telecommunications, had virtually no cases of single union representation.

9. This change, if it did occur, predated the use of the threat of withdrawal of check-off facilities that some employers made in some disputes in 1993. It also pre-dated the requirement for three-yearly confirmation of the arrangement by union members specified in the Trade Union Reform and Employment Rights Act 1993.

# 4 Single union agreements, disputes procedures and management control

Having established in the previous chapter the extent of single union representation, the types of workplace in which it was more commonly present, the unions involved and something of the nature of employee representation in single union workplaces, we now move on to consider some of the newer industrial relations practices associated with single union representation that attracted public attention in the 1980s. In so far as one element of the 'new industrial relations' was the introduction of 'single union agreements' (with various associated features which we consider later in this chapter) were such agreements really new? Was the granting of sole representation or negotiating rights to the union in question a genuine innovation on the British industrial relations scene, or was it something that had been widespread for many years but rarely commented on?

Our focus in most of this analysis is on workplaces with a single recognised trade union. We are thus leaving out of consideration the quite substantial number of workplaces with members of a single trade union which did not have full recognition for negotiating purposes. Unions in most of these, as we showed in the last chapter, simply had small numbers of members present and no formal role for the union in workplace procedures or employee representation. For much of our discussion we also exclude public sector workplaces. This hardly affects the picture at all because multi-unionism was so widespread in the public trading sector that there were virtually no workplaces in it that had members of just one recognised trade union.

## Sole union agreements in workplaces with a single recognised union

To establish the existence of single union agreements in the very broadest sense, and hence measure their extent, we asked managers in workplaces with a single recognised union, 'Do you have a formal agreement with the union to recognise *only that union* or has it just worked out that way?' To distinguish them from other uses of the term 'single union agreement' we denote such agreements with the phrase 'sole union agreements'. The overall result from our 1990 survey was that 42 per cent of workplaces in industry and commerce with a single recognised trade union had a formal sole union agreement.[1] In the 'unionised sector' (among workplaces with recognised unions) sole union agreements accounted for 23 per cent of workplaces. In industry and commerce as a whole, establishments with a formal sole union agreement accounted for 9 per cent of all workplaces and employed 10 per cent of employees.

Workplaces with sole union agreements were heavily concentrated in two industries, retail distribution and banking and insurance. In fact these two industries accounted for a half of workplaces with sole union agreements. The remainder were widely spread. Contrary to the impression given by the literature on single union deals, the number of cases in manufacturing was small and spread across all types of manufacturing. To understand why this should be so, we now focus on workplaces with a single recognised union and look at the types of employer and the types of union that were especially likely to have such agreements, rather than having a single recognised union without such an agreement.

### *Employer characteristics associated with sole union agreements*
Compared with the generality of workplaces with a single recognised union, two manufacturing industries had a notably higher incidence of sole union agreements – electrical engineering and food, drink and tobacco. The figure in vehicle manufacturing was also high but based on a very small number of cases (most unionised plants in the industry being multi-union). In service industries there was just one sector with a high incidence of agreements: the banking, insurance and financial services sector.

We examined a number of other characteristics, besides their industrial activity, to see whether they were associated with the incidence of agreements. Many of the results are given in Table 4.1. The least likely places to have them were small workplaces and small independent firms, both being associated with informality in employee relations generally. Amongst workplaces belonging to larger, multi-site organisations, sole union agreements were more likely where policy on trade union recognition was centralised at head office. Indeed, agreements were nearly twice as common in workplaces where managers reported that head office decided union recognition policy as where they reported that it was an establishment level decision; the respective proportions were 55 and 27 per cent. The presence of an on-site specialist personnel or industrial relations manager was also strongly associated with sole union agreements, rather than just the presence of a single recognised union.

**Table 4.1  The extent of formal sole union agreements in workplaces with a single recognised union, 1990**

|  | Sole union agreement | *Unweighted base* | *Percentages*<br>*Weighted base* |
|---|---|---|---|
| All private sector establishments | 42 | *286* | *314* |
| **Sector** |  |  |  |
| Manufacturing | 37 | *122* | *99* |
| Services | 44 | *164* | *215* |
| **Ownership** |  |  |  |
| Single, independent establishment | (19) | *36* | *54*[1] |
| Part of larger group | 47 | *250* | *259* |
| Foreign-owned | (48) | *31* | *31* |
| UK multi-national | 50 | *113* | *104* |
| UK national | 34 | *125* | *167* |
| **Where union recognition policy decided** |  |  |  |
| Workplace decision | 27 | *74* | *52* |
| Workplace recommendation, higher-level approval | (38) | *46* | *54* |
| Higher level, e.g. Head Office | 55 | *127* | *152* |
| **Workforce composition** |  |  |  |
| More than 70% female | 64 | *50* | *58* |
| 70% or less female | 36 | *186* | *223* |
| More than 70% non-manual | 61 | *74* | *84* |
| 70% or less non-manual | 35 | *212* | *226* |
| **Age of workplace (years)** |  |  |  |
| 21 or more | 42 | *146* | *172* |
| 10 to 20 | 45 | *73* | *76* |
| Less than 10 | 39 | *64* | *69* |
| Original new workplaces | (27) | *13* | *14* |
| Recent movers | (46) | *39* | *40* |

Base:  private sector workplaces with a single recognised union

1.  See Note H.

Foreign-owned workplaces were only slightly more likely to have a sole union agreement than UK-owned ones. The figures were 48 per cent compared with 40 per cent. Reflecting the preponderance of UK-owned workplaces generally and, more precisely, those having a single recognised trade union, our 1990 survey results showed that workplaces with sole union agreements were very largely UK owned and not predominantly foreign-owned. This contrasts sharply with studies of single union agreements reported in the specialist press.[2]

Largely reflecting their industrial distribution mentioned above, agreements were substantially more common where the workforce was predominantly female and predominantly non-manual. In workplaces with sole union agreements 48 per cent of the workforce was female; in those with a single recognised union but without such an agreement the proportion was 36 per cent. Non-manual workers comprised 47 per cent of the workforce in the former, compared with 37 per cent in the latter. Some might wish to interpret those differences as an indication of a more compliant workforce in situations where sole union agreements had been reached. We have no direct evidence that bears on such a speculation.

The most notable characteristic of workplaces that was not associated with the incidence of agreements was their age. Older workplaces were just as likely to have such agreements as younger ones. Thus the starting point of the 'new industrial relations' as generally understood, exclusive bargaining rights for a single trade union, was by no means a special feature of workplaces that came into existence in the 1980s. But had these older workplaces introduced a sole union agreement recently, after previously having multiple unions or an informal single union situation? This seems most unlikely. First of all, moves from multi-union to single union representation have been rare, as we showed earlier. Secondly, although we did not ask a specific question about when the agreement was made, we do have evidence from more general questions in the 1990 WIRS about the timing of union recognition agreements. By confining our attention to workplaces with a single recognised union it was clear from these questions that the vast majority of sole union recognition agreements pre-dated 1984. In the case of unions that had all or mostly manual members, only 6 per cent of older workplaces had made their sole union agreement within the last six years; for non-manual unions the proportion was 12 per cent. There can be little doubt that recognition agreements granting sole bargaining rights were common long before the 'new-style agreements' of the 1980s.

An additional result of our analysis with respect to the age of workplaces also went against the common belief that sole union agreements were a feature of new workplaces. Original new workplaces (established between 1984 and 1990) were *less* likely than recent movers to have formal sole union agreements. The number of observations on which this result is based is unfortunately small. However, the difference was mirrored in the results from our supplementary sample of new workplaces, also too small to be decisive on its own. But putting the two pieces of evidence together makes us reasonably confident in saying that recent movers with a single recognised union were more likely to have a formal sole union agreement than original new workplaces.

## Union characteristics associated with sole union agreements

We saw in Chapter 3 that one of the features of union representation in workplaces with a single recognised union was the degree to which it frequently involved substantial portions of the workforce being excluded from collective agreements with management. Sole union agreements appeared to do this to a much lesser extent. When we compared workplaces having a sole union agreement with those that had a single recognised union but no formal agreement for sole representation, 53 per cent of the former had a union which only represented manual or non-manual employees but not both. The comparable figure for the latter was 73 per cent.[3] Thus sole union agreements were rather less likely to leave a major section of the workforce out of account.

The pattern was similar when we looked at the coverage of collective bargaining within workplaces having the two types of single unionism. The coverage of collective bargaining in workplaces with sole union agreements was 70 per cent.[4] In single union workplaces without such agreements it was 59 per cent (Table 4.2). In younger workplaces the difference was, if anything, more pronounced: the figure for coverage was 75 per cent in younger workplaces with sole union agreements, compared with 49 per cent for those without. Thus the newer sole union agreements cover a larger proportion of employees in workplaces that have them than the generality of workplaces with a single recognised trade union.

However, this wider coverage was not reflected in higher levels of union membership. Union density was only slightly higher in single union workplaces with a sole union agreement (59 per cent compared with 52 per cent). Sole union agreements thus entail larger numbers of free riders, rather than lifting the level of membership.

A second point of interest on sole union agreements is which trade unions were involved. In descending order of frequency they were: USDAW (22 per cent of cases), BIFU (15 per cent), TGWU (12 per cent), GMB (8 per cent), EETPU (5 per cent), MSF (5 per cent) and AEU (3 per cent). Of these it is probably EETPU, AEU, TGWU and GMB that are associated in the public mind with 'single union deals'. If we simply concentrate on the question of sole representation rights these four unions were not the ones most extensively involved.

Furthermore, our analysis showed that staff associations accounted for most of the remaining 30 per cent of cases where there was a sole union

**Table 4.2  Features of trade union representation in workplaces with a single recognised union, 1990**

|  | Sole union agreement | No formal agreement |
|---|---|---|
| | | *Mean percentage of employees* |
| Coverage of collective bargaining (%) | 70 | 59 |
| Membership density (%) | 59 | 52 |
| | | *Percentage of establishments* |
| Union representative present | 69 | 64 |
| Check-off | 86 | 71 |
| Base: trading sector establishments with a single recognised union | | |
| *Unweighted base* | *136* | *124* |
| *Weighted base* | *131* | *160* |

agreement. The staff associations being discussed here were ones that were certified as being independent of their employer by the Certification Officer for Trade Unions and Employers' Associations and recognised for bargaining purposes by the employer with whom they dealt. On this basis we treated them as equivalent to trade unions in our survey interviews. They occurred almost wholly within the financial services sector, mostly in banking, where there were also substantial numbers of workplaces with sole union agreements with either BIFU or (less commonly) MSF. But whereas all the seven trade unions mentioned in the previous paragraph were involved in sole representation agreements in some workplaces and single union representation without such agreements in others, the staff associations were present in single union situations only where there was such an agreement. Thus staff associations were much more commonly involved in agreements with management not to grant recognition to their obvious rivals – trade unions. This gives some support to the common view that staff associations are sometimes used by management as a defence against the possibility of trade union representation.

To shed some light on the nature of union organisation within workplaces with sole union agreements, we examined the degree to which they had local representatives and check-off arrangements. As Table 4.2 shows, they were slightly more likely to have a local representative at the workplace and substantially more likely to have check-off. On these two indicators, then, union organisation was possibly stronger in workplaces

**Table 4.3** **Proportion of establishments with recognised unions for manual workers where each of six issues was negotiated with management, 1990**

*Percentages*

| | Number of recognised unions | |
| | 1 | 2 or more |
| --- | --- | --- |
| **Issue:** | | |
| Physical working conditions | 68 | 81 |
| Reployment within establishment | 42 | 68 |
| Staffing levels | 26 | 50 |
| Size of redundancy pay | 40 | 47 |
| Recruitment | 17 | 24 |
| Reorganisation of working hours | 75 | 89 |
| Base: trading sector establishments with recognised unions for manual workers | | |
| *Unweighted* | *225* | *547* |
| *Weighted* | *236* | *208* |

with sole union agreements than in single union workplaces without such agreements.

We also examined whether a number of other issues besides pay were dealt with through negotiations with the union. Six issues – physical working conditions, the redeployment of workers, staffing levels, recruitment, the reorganisation of working hours and the size of redundancy payments – were asked about in relation to the largest manual negotiating unit and the largest non-manual negotiating unit. Table 4.3 shows the results for workplaces with manual negotiating units (or a single union wholly or predominantly representing manual workers). The picture for the six different issues is broadly the same. In workplaces with a single union the issue was less likely to be the subject of negotiation than was the case in multi-union workplaces. Where there was a single recognised trade union, negotiation over these issues was more likely if there was a sole union agreement. The same pattern was evident when we examined the equivalent results covering non-manual negotiating units.

On the other hand, our more focused questions on technical and organisational change over the previous three years yielded a different pattern. Where new plant, machinery or equipment had been introduced, almost no managers in workplaces with a sole union agreement reported that the change had been 'negotiated with union representatives and dependent on their agreement'. Similarly, in workplaces with a sole union agreement managers were less likely to report that substantial changes in work organisation or working methods had been negotiated and agreed with union representatives than was the case in single-union workplaces without a formal, sole-union agreement. Admittedly our evidence on these two latter questions is based on smaller numbers of observations because not all workplaces had experienced these types of change recently. So these two further indicators of union influence upon management action and decisions give no unambiguous message as to whether workplaces with sole union agreements have stronger or weaker union organisation than other single-union workplaces.

### Dispute avoidance and resolution in sole union agreements

One of the features of the single union deals of the 1980s which appeared to represent a genuine innovation in British industrial relations was the inclusion in some of them of 'final-offer' or 'pendulum' arbitration as a mechanism of last resort in collective bargaining. In some cases this involved an explicit 'no-strike' undertaking by the trade union. At the time of designing our 1990 survey the known incidence of agreements including both of these two elements was very small and it was considered inappropriate to use a national sample survey to identify such cases. However, given that a section of questions on the nature of disputes procedures has always been a core element in the WIRS series, the addition of a small number of additional questions on arbitration procedures was felt appropriate. These enable us to document the overall incidence of pendulum arbitration procedures and give a broad picture of the industrial relations settings within which they occur. However, in so far as the most tightly-drawn version of these procedures commit the parties to accepting the arbitrator's judgment, they can be broadly interpreted as an agreement to avoid industrial action.

As we shall see, the existence of pendulum arbitration goes beyond the narrow confines of the sole union agreement, which has been the context in which such procedures have generally been studied.[5]

The starting point for our discussion is the type of procedure we are considering. We are not concerned here with procedures for resolving individual grievances or disputes about disciplinary matters. We are focusing on collective disputes over pay and conditions of employment. As commonly understood these arise in circumstances where pay is negotiated between management and unions. Our initial question was addressed to managers and asked whether their establishment had a formal procedure for dealing with disputes over pay and conditions of any group of workers. As Table 4.4 shows, in workplaces without recognised unions managers still frequently reported such a procedure; from the responses to later questions we interpreted this as meaning that there was an internal management procedure for reassessing proposed changes to pay if consultation with employees indicated dissatisfaction with the proposal. For current purposes we leave such cases aside and concentrate on procedures in workplaces with recognised trade unions, in other words *negotiating procedures*. It is here that arbitration is most relevant.

Negotiating procedures, as broadly defined by our first question, were less common among single union workplaces than among multi-union workplaces (73 per cent compared with 94 per cent). However, workplaces with a sole union agreement were almost as likely as multi-union workplaces to have a negotiating procedure; 90 per cent did so.

The pattern was similar when we looked at those procedures that were formally written down and agreed by both parties. Workplaces with sole union agreements were similar to multi-union workplaces; 80 per cent and 86 per cent of them, respectively, had a formal agreed procedure. It was single union workplaces without a sole union agreement that were least likely to have an agreed negotiating procedure.

Provisions for arbitration were a common but not universal feature of negotiating procedures. In broad terms one half of workplaces with agreed negotiating procedures had provision for an independent third party to arbitrate if the earlier stages of the procedure did not produce a solution. (By an independent third party we mean a person or body not belonging to the management of the enterprise and not a trade union officer. Most commonly, independent arbitration was specified as being provided through ACAS, but there were also other arrangements involving individuals or specified arbitrating bodies.) Overall, then, 37 per cent of workplaces with recognised trade unions had an agreed negotiating procedure with provision for independent arbitration. Here workplaces with sole union agreements were distinctive. Half of them had this type of procedure compared with a third of other kinds of unionised workplace.

However, having a provision for independent arbitration is still a long way from having pendulum arbitration. For one thing, access to the arbitration procedure may not be equally available to both parties. Typically, if management is able to veto the resort to arbitration, the provision is likely to be of limited value in dispute resolution. Two further questions about arbitration provisions were therefore asked to ascertain if the resort to arbitration was automatic when the earlier stages had been exhausted or, if not, whether it allowed either party to make unilateral reference to arbitration. If either of these two conditions applied we classified the procedure as having arbitration which was *accessible to both parties*. Overall, 13 per cent of workplaces with recognised unions had such

Table 4.4   Procedures for resolving pay disputes by type of union representation, 1990

*Percentages*

| | All trading sector | Number of recognised unions | | | Single union representation | |
| --- | --- | --- | --- | --- | --- | --- |
| | | None | 1 | 2 or more | Sole union agreement | No formal agreement |
| **Proportion of workplaces with:** | | | | | | |
| Pay disputes procedure | 61 | 46 | 73 | 94 | 90 | 61 |
| Procedure is written and agreed with unions | 31 | 2 | 66 | 86 | 80 | 54 |
| Agreed procedure provides for independent arbitration | 15 | 1 | 39 | 35 | 50 | 31 |
| Independent arbitration is accessible to both parties | 5 | * | 12 | 13 | 11 | 12 |
| Equally accessible arbitration is binding | 2 | – | 3 | 9 | 3 | 4 |
| Equally accessible arbitration is pendulum arbitration | 1 | – | 3 | 3 | 6 | – |
| Equally accessible arbitration is binding, pendulum arbitration | * | – | * | 2 | * | – |
| Base: trading sector workplaces specified in column headings | | | | | | |
| *Unweighted* | *1510* | *607* | *289* | *614* | *136*[1] | *124* |
| *Weighted* | *1452* | *868* | *315* | *269* | *131* | *160* |

1.   See Note G.

a procedure. There were no differences between single and multi-union workplaces, nor between the two types of single union workplace that we identified (Table 4.4, fourth row).

For arbitration to be effective in resolving disputes or encouraging a settlement earlier in the negotiating process, there needs to be a commitment by both parties to honour the outcome of the arbitration. Indeed, ACAS, the main provider of arbitration services in Britain, puts this as a defining condition.[6] To capture this feature of negotiating procedures we asked, 'does the provision specify that the decision of the arbitrator or arbitrating body must be final and binding on all parties?' Roughly a half of negotiating procedures with arbitration accessible to both parties (accounting for 6 per cent of workplaces with recognised unions) had this feature, binding arbitration. Surprisingly, since agreements are generally easier to reach if they involve fewer parties or factions, it was more common in multi-union workplaces than those with a single recognised union. The incidence of binding arbitration was no higher in single union workplaces that had a sole union agreement.

Our final question on negotiating procedures explicitly aimed to identify pendulum arbitration. Managers who had already identified a procedure with provision for arbitration were asked, 'does the arbitrator or arbitrating body have to find wholly in favour of one party or another?' This produced even fewer positive responses; overall, 3 per cent of managers in workplaces with recognised unions said their negotiating procedure had this provision (Table 4.4, sixth row). This 3 per cent, however, were not all cases where the procedure specified that the arbitrator's decision was final and binding on both management and union. If we add this condition, the incidence of full-blown pendulum arbitration was as shown in the seventh line of Table 4.4. A mere 1 per cent of workplaces with recognised unions had it.

Before discussing pendulum arbitration further, let us remind ourselves of the features that we have specified before a negotiating procedure fits our definition. The procedure had to be written and agreed by management and the union or unions and it had to provide for arbitration which:

- was independent,
- equally accessible to both parties,
- binding on both parties, and
- involved finding wholly in favour of one party or the other.

The evidence from our 1990 main sample was that pendulum arbitration, thus defined, was extremely rare. None of the cases where it was reported were single union workplaces without a sole union agreement. In workplaces with a sole union agreement, less than 1 per cent had pendulum arbitration. In multi-union workplaces 2 per cent of cases reported it. On this basis it seems to be less of a feature of the 'new style agreements' than has generally been assumed. But this is largely because previous studies have examined pendulum arbitration only in cases already identified through having a 'single union deal' or 'new-style' agreement.

With so few cases of it, not a great deal more can usefully be said about the incidence of pendulum arbitration. None of the 41 new workplaces in our supplementary sample had full-blown pendulum arbitration.[7] Nor in our main sample was it especially a feature of younger workplaces. In fact most of the very small number of workplaces with it were long established. Moreover, the rare examples of it were spread beyond the small range of industries, regions and unions in which 'single union deals' have been concentrated. We can be fairly confident in concluding that, amongst the generality of workplaces in British industry and commerce, pendulum arbitration is not a novel practice. We can be extremely confident in concluding that it remains rare.

## Union constraints upon management in the organisation of work

Besides sole union representation rights and pendulum arbitration, the third key feature of the 'new-style agreements' was an explicit undertaking by the union that management was free to organise work in any way it thought appropriate. Indeed, this was the most common of the five features of the single-union deals included in the recent study by Industrial Relations Services.[8] The targets of these arrangements were principally the demarcations between occupational groups exemplified by skilled craftsmen and union-negotiated manning levels.

We included two questions in the 1990 WIRS in order to capture the range of constraints that managers felt they faced in organising work. The first of these asked, 'In practice is management here able to organise work as it wishes among non-managerial employees or are there limits to the way it can organise work?' Those who replied that there were limits were asked, 'What limits the way management can organise the work here?' They were shown a card with seven possible options, plus the opportunity to suggest others. The results were reported in a general manner in our earlier volume and the high incidence of reported constraints of all types in the public sector of the economy was highlighted. Here our attention is on the trading sector of the economy, including some public sector workplaces but clearly dominated by private ownership. We also focus almost exclusively on the limits to management freedom of action arising from the presence of trade unions. The three types of 'union constraint' prompted in our question were as follows:

- Formal agreements with trade unions
- Opposition from shop stewards or representatives
- Opposition from ordinary union members.

No additional type of union constraint was suggested among the 'other answers' given by some respondents.

In workplaces in the trading sector of the economy that recognised trade unions, 28 per cent of managers reported any of the above three 'union constraints' in the way work was organised. Put the other way, in 72 per cent of workplaces with recognised unions the presence of trade union representation imposed no obstacles to the way management organised the work, according to the reports of managers. Thus freedom from trade union constraints in terms of work organisation, an explicit feature of the 'new union deals', appears to be widespread and hardly confined to such situations. We turn to this issue directly after making some general remarks about the pattern of our results.

First of all, it was striking that the most common type of union constraint was a formal agreement with a trade union or unions (Table 4.5). This was mentioned in over fourth fifths of the cases where any union constraint was reported. However, managers often also reported opposition from either union representatives or union members in such cases. In fact, this was so in a half of cases. This implies that many if not most of the joint union-management agreements enjoyed the support of the current workforce, rather than simply being relics of a previous era of industrial relations. But we will examine this question further a little later.

A second point of interest is that in unionised workplaces other constraints on management's ability to organise work, that is constraints unrelated to unions, were just as common as union-related constraints. Managers in 28 per cent of unionised workplaces reported them, exactly the same proportion as reported union constraints.

The characteristics of workplaces mostly strongly associated with union constraints were features of union organisation. In particular there was a sharp distinction between single union and multi-union workplaces. The former were much less likely to inhibit management in the way they organised work; the reported proportions were 16 and 43 per cent respectively. As Table 4.5 shows, the differences were apparent for all three separate types of constraint as well as for union constraints in general. A second feature of trade union representation associated with constraints on management's freedom to organise work activities was the number of negotiating groups involved. Where there was a single negotiating group, 15 per cent of managers reported union constraints; in those with two or more negotiating groups the figure was 45 per cent. These two features of

**Table 4.5  Constraints on management's ability to organise work in unionised workplaces, 1990**

*Percentages*

| Type of constraint | All unionised workplaces | Number of recognised unions | | | | |
|---|---|---|---|---|---|---|
| | | 1 | 2 | 3 | 4 | 5 or more |
| Formal agreement with trade union | 24 | 13 | 39 | 31 | 34 | 35 |
| Opposition from union representatives | 12 | 4 | 23 | 21 | 20 | 25 |
| Opposition from union members | 10 | 5 | 14 | 20 | 17 | 25 |
| Any union constraint | 28 | 16 | 46 | 35 | 40 | 45 |
| Any non-union constraint | 28 | 28 | 29 | 25 | 18 | 42 |
| Any constraint | 41 | 35 | 48 | 41 | 44 | 67 |
| No limits on management freedom to organise work | 59 | 65 | 52 | 59 | 56 | 33 |

Base: trading sector establishments with recognised unions

| | | | | | | |
|---|---|---|---|---|---|---|
| *Unweighted* | *903* | *291* | *188* | *116* | *146* | *162* |
| *Weighted* | *584*[1] | *316* | *165* | *52* | *25* | *25* |

1. See Note H.

**Table 4.6**  Union constraints on management flexibility in relation to number of unions and number of negotiating units, 1990

*Percentages*

| Proportion of workplaces where managers reported any union constraint on management's ability to organise work | Number of negotiating units | | |
|---|---|---|---|
| | 1 | 2 | 3 or more |
| **Number of recognised unions** | | | |
| 1 | 15 | (28) | § |
| 2 | (15) | 47 | (74) |
| 3 or more | (36) | 23 | 43 |

Base: trading sector establishments with recognised unions

union representation appeared to dominate the pattern of results and clearly required further attention in the context of our current discussion of single union agreements. Table 4.6 shows how these two features of union representation were associated with union constraints. It carries no clear message other than that the simplest form of representation – one union and one bargaining unit – was the arrangement least associated with union constraints. In cases where two unions negotiated jointly, union constraints upon management's organisation of work were also uncommon; but, as we showed earlier, such cases were rare.

Single union representation, then, was strongly associated with managerial freedom in the organisation of work. But was this freedom a feature of sole union agreements or of other characteristics of workplaces and their systems of union representation?

## *Management freedom in single union workplaces*

The simple and possibly surprising message from our survey results was that, among single union workplaces, those with a sole union agreement were much *less* likely to report management freedom to organise work. In fact, 24 per cent of workplaces with sole union agreements reported union constraints, compared with only 6 per cent of single union workplaces without a formal agreement to recognise only the one union. Nevertheless, over three quarters of managers in workplaces with sole union agreements reported complete freedom to organise work. In this sense the 'single union deals' of the 1980s were not at all unusual. They simply reflected the common reality of the widespread lack of union influence in the sphere of work organisation.

Besides the lack of a sole union agreement, three other features of single union workplaces stood out in terms of managerial freedom in the organisation of work. The first of these was ownership. UK-owned workplaces were more likely to report managerial freedom from union constraints than foreign-owned workplaces (Table 4.7). Contrary to the impressions given by reports of single union deals, foreign-owned workplaces were more than twice as likely to report union constraints than indigenously owned sites. The differences were apparent for all three types of constraint: formal agreements with unions, opposition from union representatives and opposition from ordinary union members.

The second, and less unexpected relationship, was with union membership density. Management freedom to organise work was much more common in workplaces with low levels of union membership. Indeed, it was almost universal in workplaces where less than half of the workforce belonged to the union.

Thirdly, and again no matter for surprise, management freedom was much more a feature of younger workplaces. Only 9 per cent of younger workplaces (those established from 1984 onwards) reported any union constraints on the organisation of work, compared with 17 per cent of older workplaces. Furthermore, among younger workplaces it was only among movers that formal agreements with unions about work organisation were reported. None of the original new workplaces reported such agreements; but they did report higher levels of potential opposition from union representatives and union members. Our base for comparisons is rather small here,[9] but these results do suggest that union constraints on management freedom become transformed, as establishments grow older, from individualised opposition to collectively recognised constraints embodied in agreements with management.

Further analysis of the interrelationships of these various characteristics of workplaces and the existence of union constraints on management flexibility in the organisation of work led us to a number of conclusions. First of all, union constraints were more common in older workplaces, whether or not there was a sole union agreement. Secondly, union constraints were increasingly likely the greater the proportion of the workforce that belonged to the union, again irrespective of whether there was a sole union agreement. Put another way, when we compared single union workplaces of similar ages or similar levels of union membership, union constraints were more common in workplaces with a sole union agreement.

In general, then, and contrary to the impression given by looking only at 'single union deals', sole union agreements appear more likely to exist

**Table 4.7  Union constraints on management flexibility in single union workplaces, 1990**

*Percentages*

| | Type of union constraint: | | | | |
| | Any | Formal agreement | Opposition from representatives or members | Unweighted base | Weighted base |
|---|---|---|---|---|---|
| **Proportion of workplaces where managers reported constraint** | | | | | |
| All single union workplaces | 16 | 13[1] | 7 | 289 | 315 |
| Sole union agreement | 24 | 20 | 11 | 136[2] | 131 |
| No sole union agreement | 6 | 5 | 1 | 124 | 160 |
| UK owned | 14 | 12 | 5 | 240 | 272 |
| Foreign owned | (31) | (25) | 19 | 31 | 31 |
| **Union membership density** | | | | | |
| Less than 50 per cent | 6 | 2 | 4 | 105 | 111 |
| 50 to 74 per cent | 18 | 18 | 1 | 70 | 95 |
| 75 per cent or more | 21 | 18 | 13 | 85 | 84 |
| **Age of establishment** | | | | | |
| Up to 10 years | 7 | 4 | 3 | 72 | 79 |
| 11 to 20 years | 21 | 18 | 15 | 69 | 64 |
| 21 or more years | 18 | 15 | 5 | 142 | 165 |

Base: trading sector establishments with one recognised trade union

1. See Note E.
2. See Note G.

in situations of relatively strong trade unionism than single unionism *per se* and are less likely to be accompanied by complete freedom on the part of management to organise work in whatever way it thinks fit. In a substantial minority of cases, the price management has payed for avoiding multi-unionism has been to concede joint decision-making on the organisation of work.

## Types of single union representation

A final overview of single union representation is now in order. We do this by focusing on three dimensions of the union-management relationship in workplaces with a single recognised trade union. The first of these is whether the union has sole representation rights. The second is whether work organisation is subject to joint regulation. The third is the extent to which pay is jointly determined by the two parties – as indicated by the proportion of the workforce covered by a jointly negotiated pay settlement. This last dimension is simply represented by whether coverage is high (75 per cent or more) or low compared with the median for workplaces with a single recognised union.[10] Using these three dimensions, the distribution of types of single union representation is shown in the eight cells of Table 4.8.

The most common type, encompassing a third of cases, is where union power is weak and the union does not have sole representation rights. Here, the union covers relatively few workers and does not influence management in the way work is organised. Secondly, about a fifth of cases are ones where again there is no agreement on sole representation nor is there joint regulation of work, but the coverage of pay bargaining is relatively high. Presumably here the threat of another union recruiting and organising a section of the workforce is low and management have seen no need to concede sole representation rights to the union at the site.

The third and fourth most common types of single union representation each account for something approaching a fifth of cases. They are ones with a sole union agreement, but again no union influence on the organisation of work. The somewhat larger category, accounting for 18 per cent of the sample of workplaces with a single recognised union, also contains workplaces with low coverage; the union is neither powerful nor is it pervasive in its effect on pay at the site. The sole union agreement, in these cases, is with a union that does represent a substantial minority – in some cases a majority – of the workforce. But coverage is not high, either because of the union's own recruitment policy or its limited appeal, or because of management's curtailment of its coverage. Many of the well-publicised 'single union deals' fit into this category.[11] The remainder would fit into

**Table 4.8   Types of single union representation, 1990**

*Percentages of whole table*

| Union coverage for pay bargaining | Single union agreement Union constrains management? | | No single union agreement Union constrains management? | |
|---|---|---|---|---|
| | Yes | No | Yes | No |
| High (75% or more) | 11 | 16 | 2 | 19 |
| Low (less than 75%) | 0 | 18 | 2 | 33 |

Base: trading sector establishments with a single recognised union

*Unweighted base:   269*
*Weighted base:      292*

our fourth category: workplaces with a sole union agreement, no union influence on work organisation, but a high degree of coverage of collective bargaining.

The fifth type of single union representation – and the only remaining one with substantial numbers – is the case where sole representation rights are accorded to a locally powerful union, as measured by the presence of joint determination of both pay and aspects of work organisation. Roughly a tenth of our sample of workplaces with a single recognised union were of this type.

It is clear, then, that single union representation in Britain covers a wide variety of forms and that only a small minority of cases have even the most basic characteristics of the well-publicised single union deals of the 1980s. More common were cases where the union was weak, covering few employees and having no monopoly on union recruitment.[12]

It is most unlikely that this picture changed substantially during the course of the 1980s. When we confined our analysis to workplaces created in the 1980s the relative frequency of the five main types shown in Table 4.8 was indistinguishable from those for the sample as a whole – except for one thing. There were many fewer cases with unions having substantial power at workplace level, based on our two indicators of joint decision making over work organisation and over pay for a high proportion of the workforce. Our supplementary sample of new workplaces also lent weight to this conclusion. The compensating increase in the single-union population was in workplaces with a weak union. But the variety of types of single unionism persisted and certainly the picture did not move towards one dominated by the single union agreements that came to prominence in the 1980s.

## Notes and references

1. Non-response to this question amounted to 7 per cent and 'other answers' totalled less than half of one per cent. For present purposes we have reclassified non-respondents with those replying 'it just worked out that way'. This was largely because the workplace in question were mostly older workplace and, as we shall see later, had long-standing recognition agreements.

2. In the results of a recent postal survey of 'single union deals', Industrial Relations Services (IRS) reported that the vast majority of plants in the survey were owned by foreign companies. The survey was based on a sample compiled from a number of lists of 'new-style agreements', most of which pre-dated our 1990 survey, and they also mostly post-dated the census on which our 1990 survey was based. The criterion for inclusion in the IRS survey was that the organisation had made a 'single union deal', by which was meant, 'a package of measures ... including some (sic) or all of the following elements: sole bargaining rights for one union; single status for manual and staff employees;...' From the tabulated results it appears that two criteria for inclusion were used: sole bargaining rights for one union; and one or more of the five other elements (single status, company council, full flexibility, pendulum arbitration or a no-strike deal). Thus the IRS study was based on a tighter definition of single union agreement than the one we are currently considering here. This, the study's response rate of 25 per cent, and many other factors no doubt account for the difference concerning the involvement of foreign companies in such agreements. See Industrial Relations Services (1993), 'Single-union deals Survey:1', *Employment Trends,* No.528, pp.3-15.

3. These comparisons were confined to workplaces with both manual and non-manual employees.

4. It should be noted that a small number of workplaces with a single union had two negotiating units, usually separate ones for manual and non-manual employees. This increased the likelihood of coverage being extensive in such cases.

5. The most recent and detailed study of pendulum arbitration in Britain is by Simon Milner, *Final-Offer Arbitration in the UK: Incidence, Processes and Outcomes,* Employment Department, London, 1993.

6. ACAS (1990) *Employment Handbook,* p.11.

7. One case had a procedure with independent, binding arbitration; another had pendulum arbitration that was non-binding. But there was no case with both of these characteristics.

8. IRS (1993) 'Single-union deals survey: 1', *Employment Trends,* No. 528, pp.3-15.

9. There were 13 original new workplaces (established in 1984 onwards) with a single recognised union in our 1990 main samples; and there were 40 movers. Workplaces with a single recognised union were too few in our supplementary sample for the results on questions confined to them to be reported.

10. The precise median was 72 per cent.

11. Just over half of the single union deals reported in the IRS study (*Employment Trends,* No. 528) were ones where the coverage of bargaining was restricted to shop-floor workers.

12. Interpreting the coverage of collective bargaining as an indicator of union power, while not indisputable, seems generally reasonable. It was recently found to be the single best proxy for 'union power', using variables available in the 1984 WIRS. See Pierella Paci, Adam Wagstaff and Peter Holl (1993), 'Measuring union power in British manufacturing: a latent variable approach', *Oxford Bulletin of Economics and Statistics,* vol.55, no.1, pp.65-85. The question on union constraints, also used here as an indicator of union power, was only asked of works managers in the 1984 survey and was thus not available for the whole of the manufacturing sample used for the above analysis.

# 5 Employee involvement and HRM practices

As we noted in Chapter 1, part of the 1980s debate about new forms of industrial relations concerned the rejection of traditional methods of communicating with employees via trade union channels and the adoption of more direct methods of communication and, possibly, consultation. To some commentators and practitioners any method of communication between management and employees that involved representation was simply out of tune with the growing philosophy of individualism that, in their view, was and should be a feature of the decade. In that view, as in much of the Human Resource Management literature, the way forward was through 'team briefing', company newsletters and the like. To others, channels of communication between management and employees that involved representatives on the employees' side, but not necessarily trade union representatives, were among the routes to better communication in larger workplaces. One of the features of the single union deals that received much attention was the inclusion of some sort of forum or 'Company Council' within which employee representatives could be informed and consulted by management to 'ensure that there is opportunity for genuine involvement of employees in the activities and plans of the company', to quote the EETPU's model agreement.[1] Another part of the debate concerned the use of financial reward or stake-holding to increase the identification and loyalty of employees to their employer. Public policy favoured this latter approach through tax incentives for employee share ownership and profit-sharing schemes while at the same time exhorting managements to develop a variety of forms of 'employee involvement', ones that usually omitted trade union representation.

There is much of relevance to these concerns in the evidence from successive surveys in the WIRS series. We have comparable questions from the two most recent surveys on the channels and methods of communication used by management to inform and consult with employees, as well as data on some of the forms of 'financial participation'. As with our earlier discussion of trade union representation, our purpose here is to extend the analysis contained in the initial volume on the 1990 survey by looking in more detail at the sources of change and the extent of innovatory practices.

We begin by examining the shrinkage in the extent of channels of communication using employee representatives, noted in the earlier volume.[2] Again our focus here is on industry and commerce in the period 1984 to 1990, because it is for that sector of the economy that we can bring all the sources of information from the WIRS series to bear.

Our initial indicator of whether a workplace had a formal channel of communication between management and employees was derived from a question addressed to managers asking whether their workplace had a joint committee of managers and employees primarily concerned with consultation.[3] However, since the mere existence of such a committee or 'council' might include a few cases where it hardly functioned in any real sense, for present purposes we have added two further conditions before including it as a 'functioning committee'. These were taken from the answers to two questions about the principal (or only) consultative committee: how frequently it had met in the past year and what, if any, important issues (in the eyes of management) it had discussed. We defined a 'functioning consultative committee' as one that met at least once every three months and had discussed important issues in management's view within the last year.[4] As the first two columns in Table 5.1 show, on this definition the proportion of workplaces in industry and commerce with a functioning consultative committee fell from 24 per cent to 18 per cent between 1984 and 1990, a fall of one quarter.

Comparison with the broader definition, simply whether a committee was reported, shows that the decline in the incidence of consultative committees or councils was not because there were fewer that existed in name only. Such cases were equally uncommon at the two points in time. So the weeding out of token committees can be ruled out as an explanation for the decline in their incidence. Functioning consultative committees certainly became less common. The following analysis refers throughout to committees defined thus, as detailed in the previous paragraph.

A second, more substantial, line of explanation might be that managements were disbanding this type of communication channel, possibly in favour of other methods. Our panel data showed that this was not the case. The number of panel cases that moved from having a consultative committee in 1984 to not having one in 1990 was almost exactly matched by the number of cases changing in the opposite direction. Moreover, workplaces that abandoned consultative committees were similar in most respects to those that introduced them, at least in terms of industrial composition, size, age, ownership, union representation and so on. The results did suggest that workplaces introducing a consultative committee were more likely to be ones that had increased substantially in size during the period, which gives some support for the notion that formal channels become more necessary as workplace size increases. There was also a slightly greater tendency for foreign-owned workplaces to introduce consultative committees than for UK-owned ones to do so. However, these differences were not especially marked. The other interesting difference thrown up by our analysis was that workplaces that had abandoned their committee were more likely to have been ones that had relatively poor industrial relations and poor financial performance in 1984 in the view of our management respondents. These cases are more suggestive of changes in management behaviour in the light of adverse circumstances, perhaps accompanied by a withdrawal of attempts to consult and involve employees or by management initiatives to try methods other than formally constituted joint committees in order to involve employees in the solution of problems.

The analysis in our initial report on the 1990 survey came to the view that the decline in the incidence of consultative committees was partly, if not largely, a matter of compositional change. That is to say, the decline arose because the types of workplace most likely to have consultative committees were the types that were forming a declining proportion of the economy. The two characteristics most strongly associated with the existence of a consultative committee were a large workforce and the presence of one or more recognised trade unions. As we showed in Chapters 1 and 2, such workplaces were certainly less common in industry and commerce by 1990 than they were in 1984. But our comparison between the two years showed that consultative committees became less common in all sizes of workplace, both unionised and non-union. However, the decline in the unionised sector was generally greater overall, as Table 5.1 shows. It was also particularly concentrated in smaller, unionised workplaces, which are so much more numerous than larger ones. In fact, unionised workplaces with between 25 and 100 employees in 1990 were only about one half as likely to have a functioning consultative committee in 1990 as similar establishments were in 1984. By contrast, among the non-union workplaces in this smaller size category there was hardly a fall. Indeed, by 1990 there was no difference between union and non-union workplaces with less than 100 employees, whereas in 1984 unionised workplaces of this size had had a greater incidence of consultative committees.

In addition, the incidence of committees in the largest non-union workplaces in 1990 was greater than in the smallest non-union workplaces by a smaller margin than was the case in 1984. So, while it remained true that larger workplaces and unionised workplaces in 1990 were more likely

**Table 5.1  The extent of consultative committees at workplace level in the union and non-union sectors, 1984 and 1990**

*Percentages*

| | All establishments | | Unions recognised | | No recognised union | |
|---|---|---|---|---|---|---|
| | 1984 | 1990 | 1984 | 1990 | 1984 | 1990 |
| Consultative committee at workplace | 27 | 21 | 34 | 24 | 21 | 18 |
| Committee meets at least every 3 months | 25 | 19 | 30 | 22 | 20 | 17 |
| 'Functioning consultative committee'* | 24 | 18 | 29 | 21 | 19 | 16 |
| Base: trading sector establishments | | | | | | |
| *Unweighted* | *1385* | *1510* | *965* | *903* | *420* | *607* |
| *Weighted* | *1373* | *1452* | *710* | *584* | *663* | *868* |

\*  Defined as a consultative committee that met at least once every 3 months and discussed something important in the view of management (see text).

to have consultative committees, the 'effects' of size and unionisation appear to have diminished.

Two further aspects of the decline are worth reporting, one concerning the prevalence of consultative committees among workplaces that disappeared between 1984 and 1990, the other among those that came into existence during the period. For the first we return to our 'unproductive panel sample', comparing workplaces that had closed down between 1984 and 1990 with the whole 1984 trading sector sample. This comparison gave a clear pattern: closures were rather more likely to have been among plants that had had consultative committees in 1984. The comparable figures for the proportion of establishments with a functioning consultative committee in the terms defined above were 24 per cent of all establishments and 28 per cent for those that had closed. This relatively small difference hid rather larger differences between union and non-union workplaces. Among unionised plants in 1984, 29 per cent had a functioning consultative committee in the terms defined above; among plants that disappeared 42 per cent of them had had such a committee. By contrast, non-union plants that closed had much the same incidence of committees as all non-union plants in 1984; the figures were 15 per cent and 19 per cent respectively.[5] On this evidence it was particularly workplaces operating a dual system of representation that disappeared from the population in the late 1980s.

New workplaces were not of the type that would offset this influence upon the overall picture. Those that came into existence between 1984 and 1990 differed little from their older counterparts in terms of having joint consultative committees or similar bodies. In our 1990 survey, 19 per cent of older workplaces had such a body, compared with 15 per cent of younger workplaces (those created in 1984 or thereafter). In our small supplementary sample of new workplaces the figure was 24 per cent. Thus the true incidence among younger workplaces is no doubt somewhat higher than 15 per cent and probably indistinguishable from the figure for older workplaces (19 per cent). When we looked for differences attributable to age among workplaces of different sizes there were none except amongst larger workplaces; amongst smaller workplaces (those with less than 100 employees) older and younger workplaces had precisely the same incidence of consultative committees. Similarly, there was no difference between older and younger workplaces when we focused on the non-union sector. The greater propensity of older workplaces to have such a committee was solely a feature of workplaces with union recognition. Thus a part of the decline in the incidence of consultative committees in the late 1980s appears to be attributable to the shrinkage in the unionised sector that occurred during that time.

Even within the remaining unionised sector, trade unions appeared to be playing less of a part in consultative processes in 1990 than earlier. This was clearly evident from the answers to questions about how employee representatives on main (or only) consultative committees were chosen. Among establishments that had a functioning consultative committee and recognised trade unions in 1984, 62 per cent had some or all of the representatives on the committee chosen by the union. Among comparable workplaces in 1990 the figure was 48 per cent. Thus by 1990, even in unionised workplaces, employee representatives on consultative committees were most often selected through non-union channels.

It was evident, however, that the reduction of trade union involvement in formal consultative machinery of the type we are discussing here was not offset by a growth of committees with non-union employee representation. Functioning consultative committees with some representatives chosen through union channels were present in 9 per cent of trading sector establishment in 1984, but a mere 4 per cent in 1990. But functioning committees with no employee representatives chosen by unions did not become more common; they were present in 15 per cent of establishments in 1984 and 14 per cent in 1990. Making our comparisons in terms of numbers of employees rather than numbers of establishments gave a similar picture of the change. In fact it showed that by 1990 there were more employees in workplaces with a functioning consultative committee with no union involvement than there were in workplaces where there was a similar committee with union representatives. This was a stark reversal of the situation in 1984 and earlier. However, the fundamental change over the period was in the proportion of employees *without* access to a joint management-employee committee; this grew from 57 per cent of employees in 1984 to 70 per cent in 1990.

## The functioning of consultative committees

Before moving on to discuss what other methods of communicating with or involving employees might have emerged during the period, some brief remarks on the functioning of consultative bodies are in order. The broad picture presented in the earlier volume was one of continuity.[6] There was no substantial change in the degree to which consultative committees were involved in negotiation as well as consultation. Production and employment issues continued to be the issues most commonly cited by managers as the most important ones discussed by the committees. There was little change in the frequency with which they met or (since 1980, when this question was previously asked) in the proportion of meetings attended by senior management.

**Table 5.2    Indicators of the functioning of principal consultative committees among younger and older workplaces, 1990**

*Percentages*

|  | All trading sector | Older workplaces | Younger workplaces (0-6 years) |
|---|---|---|---|
| Proportion of establishments where principal consultative committee: | | | |
| - Met at least once a month | 52 | 48 | 73 |
| - Was attended by senior management at all meetings | 87 | 87 | 87 |
| - Was 'very influential' on management decisions | 29 | 26 | 43 |

Base: trading sector establishments with a 'functioning consultative committee' (see text)

| | | | |
|---|---|---|---|
| *Unweighted* | *521* | *464* | *57* |
| *Weighted* | *266* | *218* | *48* |

It would not be appropriate to repeat that analysis here. And in view of the overall lack of change, there is less of a case for carrying out the sort of detailed analysis that we have presented in the foregoing pages on the incidence of consultative committees. But, given the potential for practices among newer workplaces to influence the overall picture in the future, there is some interest in seeing whether newer workplaces were distinctive in the way that their consultative committees functioned. Table 5.2 gives the comparative picture from our 1990 survey for older and younger workplaces concerning three main features of the functioning of consultative committees.

On two of the three measures there appeared to be significant differences in the way that functioning consultative committees operated in younger workplaces. They met more frequently and they were more often rated by managers as 'very influential' with regard to management decision-making. Of course, managers' responses to an evaluative question about the influence of a consultative committee upon management's decisions may be regarded with some scepticism, but, as was shown in the earlier volume, there was a substantial degree of agreement between managers and employee representatives on this question.[7] It seems unlikely that our current concentration on manager's accounts is leading us to wrong conclusions about the differences between older and younger workplaces in the way committees were functioning.

The tendency for consultative committees and similar bodies in newer workplaces to meet more often and to be regarded as more influential could mean that they were enabling employees to play a more active role in management-employee relationships than was the case in older workplaces. However, two points suggest caution in such an interpretation. The first is that the greater frequency of meetings and greater apparent influence of committees in younger workplaces was solely a feature of workplaces that had moved location. New, original workplaces, established in 1984 or later, were no different from older workplaces in these two respects. Yet it is among these that we would be looking for the most distinctive behaviour if the overall picture in the trading sector were to be changing substantially.

The second point that suggests caution in interpreting the greater apparent influence of consultative committees in younger workplaces is that a more marked difference exists between committees with trade union representatives and those without. Managers were twice as likely to rate a consultative committee as 'very influential' if it contained no trade union representatives than they were when some employee representatives were chosen through union channels. Similarly, committees were rated as more influential in workplaces without recognised trade unions. In so far as collective bargaining provides an alternative channel through which employees may influence management decisions, such a difference might well be expected. Since, as we showed in Chapter 2, union recognition was substantially less common in younger workplaces, the lack of this alternative method of influencing management decisions probably accounts for much of the greater reported influence of consultative committees, where they existed, in younger workplaces than in older ones.

Before moving on to look at other channels of communication and consultation besides consultative committees, a brief word is relevant in relation to the 'new union deals' of the 1980s. As we recalled at the beginning of this chapter, one of the characteristics of these agreements was the inclusion of some sort of forum or 'Company Council' within which employee representatives could be informed and consulted by management. Such a body would clearly come within the scope of our initial question about joint committees of managers and employees, the results of which have been discussed above. As also shown above, such bodies were somewhat more common in workplaces with recognised trade unions, but were they particularly common in workplaces with a single trade union or in those with a sole union agreement? The answer to the first question is undoubtedly 'no'. Multi-union workplaces were more likely to have functioning consultative committees; 28 per cent of them did so compared with 16 per cent of workplaces with a single recognised union. On the second question there was no marked difference. Workplaces with a sole union agreement were slightly more likely to have a committee than other single union workplaces but the difference was nowhere near being statistically significant. Furthermore, if we take these two characteristics of the 'new union deals' – a sole union agreement and a functioning consultative forum – workplaces with both of these features were rare. Between 1 and 2 per cent of workplaces in industry and commerce fitted this description.

### A broader look at management-employee communication

The whole of the foregoing discussion has been concerned with a specific sort of channel of communication between management and employees, one which some have argued was losing favour in British workplaces and being replaced or supplemented by other methods, some of them more innovatory. We have spent some time discussing this particular communication channel for several reasons: partly because of its importance in the 'new-style agreements' of the 1980s; partly because our initial results showed that it became less common in the late 1980s; and partly because the comparable results from our earlier surveys had aroused academic controversy.[8] But, as we shall now show, such committees were one of the *least* common formal channels through which management communicated with and consulted employees. Were other mechanisms becoming more widely used?

In our management interviews, following on the questions about the existence and characteristics of joint committees of managers and employees concerned with consultation, we asked our respondents whether they used, as a matter of policy, any of the following methods to communicate with or consult employees.

- Regular meetings (at least once a month) between junior managers/supervisors and all the workers for whom they are responsible
- Regular meetings (at least once a year) between senior managers and all sections of the workforce
- Systematic use of the management chain for communication with all employees
- Suggestion schemes
- Regular newsletters distributed to all employees.

The question included a few additional items in both our 1984 and 1990 surveys, but the analysis here is restricted to the ones listed above because

**Table 5.3    Methods used by management to communicate with or consult employees, 1984 and 1990**

|  | Proportion of establishments | | Proportion of employees | |
|---|---|---|---|---|
|  | 1984 | 1990 | 1984 | 1990 |
|  |  |  |  | *Percentages* |
| Regular meetings with junior management | 30 | 44 | 37 | 52 |
| Regular meetings with senior management | 33 | 39 | 39 | 45 |
| Management chain of communication | 60 | 59 | 70 | 66 |
| Suggestion scheme | 25 | 27 | 35 | 38 |
| Regular newsletters | 33 | 39 | 52 | 53 |
| Functioning consultative committee | 24 | 18 | 43 | 30 |
| Any of these six methods | 84[1] | 84 | 91 | 90 |
|  |  |  |  | *Means* |
| Average number of different methods | 2.1 | 2.3 | 2.8 | 2.8 |

Base: columns 1 and 2, trading sector establishments; columns 3 and 4, employees in trading sector establishments

1.   See Note F.

they are the ones that most clearly provide a regular or enduring channel of communication between management and employees.[9]

Table 5.3 shows the extent to which the five channels of communication listed above, plus functioning consultative committees, existed in both 1984 and 1990 in British industry and commerce, according to the accounts of our management interviewees.[10] The table gives two measures: the percentage of workplaces with the specified communication channel; and the percentage of employees in such workplaces.

Whichever of these two measures is chosen, the overall picture is one of stability over the period in the use of *any* of the six methods specified. On the establishment-based measure, 84 per cent of workplaces in both surveys reported any of the six methods;[11] on the employee-based measure the proportions were also practically identical. However, when we examined the particular methods one by one, there was evidence of change. The decline in the extent of consultative committees was offset by increases in other channels of communication between management and employees.

Three methods showed an increase. The most marked growth was in regular meetings between supervisors or junior managers and their workgroup.[12] Such meetings, on a monthly or more frequent basis, were reported in 44 per cent of workplaces in 1990 compared with 30 per cent in 1984. The employee-based measure rose from 37 per cent to 52 per cent over the period. The two measures show a substantial increase in the use of a direct channel of communication between management and employees, a channel that might involve two-way communication in many cases. But we should also note the more modest rise in the extent of regular (although less frequent) meetings between senior managers and employees – as evidenced by both the establishment and the employee-based measures of extent (Table 5.3). This is also a direct, face-to-face method of communication, although more realistically with less likelihood of being two-way than is the case for meetings involving more junior management. Thirdly, management newsletters to employees became more commonly used, according to our establishment-based measure; however, on our employee-based measure there was no discernible difference between the two survey results.

Thus the first two channels of communication mentioned above clearly became more widespread, whichever measure of their extent we used. Along with the continuing use of the management chain for communicating directly with employees (and the other methods which also remained at similar levels of use) the growing extent of these two methods filled the gap left by the decline in the prevalence of formal consultative committees. Of course, the channels that had become more widespread were ones which could more easily be dominated by management and might result in little upward communication from the workforce to management. But it is noteworthy that the channel that increased in extent to the greatest degree ('briefing groups') was the one with the greatest potential for employees to play an active part.

Before looking in further detail at the changing mix of methods of communication, it is worth noting the bottom line in Table 5.3 which shows the degree to which several of the six specified communication channels were used within the same establishments. On an establishment basis, the mean number of channels rose slightly, from 2.1 to 2.3 between 1984 and 1990. However, on the alternative, employee-based measure there was no

**Table 5.4** **The extent of regular meetings between junior managers and their subordinates, 1984 and 1990**

|  | | *Percentages* |
| --- | --- | --- |
|  | 1984 | 1990 |
| All trading sector | 30 | 44 |
| Sector | | |
| Manufacturing | 25 | 31 |
| Services | 32 | 49 |
| Size of workplace | | |
| 25-99 employees | 28 | 41 |
| 100-499 | 35 | 53 |
| 500-999 | 48 | 60 |
| 1,000 or more | 44 | 77 |
| Size of enterprise | | |
| 25-500 employees | 23 | 28 |
| 500-4,999 | 39 | 40 |
| 5,000-49,999 | 41 | 55 |
| 50,000 or more | 45 | 77 |
| No information | 36 | 49 |
| Ownership | | |
| Private sector, UK-owned | 30 | 42 |
| Private sector, foreign-owned | 39 | 40 |
| Public sector | 21 | 84 |
| Union representation | | |
| Union recognised | 29 | 56 |
| No recognised union | 31 | 35 |

Base: trading sector establishments

change – the employee-weighted mean was 2.8 in both surveys.[13] Given this equivocal evidence it would be hard to argue that there was a discernible increase in the use of multiple channels of communication over the period 1984 to 1990 in industry and commerce.[14]

Returning to the incidence of particular methods of communication, our analysis concentrates on the first two methods shown in Table 5.3, these two types of meeting between management and employees being the ones to show a discernible increase in extent. Table 5.4 gives a clear indication of the types of workplace in which there was a growth in regular meetings between junior managers and their subordinates. The most marked was the public sector, where the extent of such meetings changed from 21 per cent of workplaces in 1984 to 84 per cent in 1990. Of course the public trading sector was much reduced by privatisation during the period, but this can hardly account for the change. There clearly was a very widespread adoption of this type of meeting in public sector trading organisations in the late 1980s. But the private sector also showed a substantial increase, or rather the UK-owned (majority) portion of it did. Here the increase was from 32 to 42 per cent of workplaces. It was only in foreign-owned workplaces, which had had the highest incidence of such meetings in 1984, that there was no subsequent increase. By 1990 UK and foreign-owned workplaces were on a par in respect of their use of this particular channel of communication.

Most of the other characteristics shown in Table 5.4 show changes that partly reflect those related to ownership. The greater tendency for an increase in workplaces belonging to very large organisations reflects the larger size of public sector enterprises. The greater increase in services than in manufacturing also partly reflects the concentration of public sector organisations in this sector. But the increase was not confined to the public sector or to industries which had experienced privatisation during the second half of the 1980s. It seemed to be a more general phenomenon among larger organisations, in essence those with over 5,000 employees. This suggests that the initiative for introducing meetings of this sort came from head office management or at least from management at levels above the workplace in large, multi-site enterprises.

We have no direct data about the source of such initiatives in large enterprises. Some could have arisen in response to the exhortations of management teachers and writers, professional organisations, government ministers and so on. Others may have come as a management response to commercial, competitive pressures, particularly from foreign suppliers. We cannot tell. But the fact that the initiatives were largely in workplaces with recognised trade unions is surely of major significance. In the union sector the incidence of these meetings virtually doubled (from 29 per cent in 1984 to 56 in 1990), whereas there was only a slight increase in the non-union sector. The change, then, can perhaps most readily be interpreted as coming from top management in large organisations and one designed to supplement or partially replace trade unions as one of the principal channels of communication between management and employees. This interpretation adds substance to the widely held (but somewhat contentious) view that the 1980s saw a reassertion by management in the unionised sector of the British economy of its control over communications with the workforce.

A quite different pattern of change emerged from our results concerning the second channel of communication between management and employees

**Table 5.5  The extent of regular meetings between senior managers and all the workforce, 1984 and 1990**

| | | *Percentages* |
|---|---|---|
| | 1984 | 1990 |
| All trading sector | 33 | 39 |
| Sector | | |
| Manufacturing | 37 | 38 |
| Services | 32 | 39 |
| Size of workplace | | |
| 25-99 employees | 32 | 37 |
| 100-499 | 35 | 46 |
| 500-999 | 47 | 52 |
| 1,000 or more | 54 | 56 |
| Size of organisation | | |
| 25-500 employees | 29 | 35 |
| 500-4,999 | 31 | 38 |
| 5,000-49,999 | 42 | 45 |
| 50,000 or more | 41 | 48 |
| No information | 43 | 39 |
| Ownership | | |
| Private sector, UK-owned | 33 | 39 |
| Private sector, foreign-owned | 45 | 44 |
| Public sector | 25 | 25 |
| Union representation | | |
| Unions recognised | 37 | 40 |
| No recognised unions | 29 | 38 |

that exhibited an increase between 1984 and 1990. Regular meetings between *senior* managers and all sections of the workforce became significantly more common only in the non-union sector (Table 5.5). Here the proportion of workplaces where such meetings occurred at least once a year rose from 29 to 38 per cent. (In unionised workplaces the change was from 37 to 40 per cent and barely significant.) The growth was again confined to service industries, but only among UK-owned private sector enterprises. The change was apparent (but not large) among both large and small workplaces and among enterprises of different sizes. The concentration within the non-union sector of the growth in this predominantly 'top-down' channel of communication was the clearest feature of the results.

In broad terms the changing extent and mix of channels used by management to communicate with employees can be summarised as follows. In the unionised sector of the economy there was a substantial contraction in the incidence of joint consultative committees and in the role of trade unions in the minority of workplaces where such committees continued to exist. Instead, managements increasingly used more direct methods of communication, particularly regular meetings between junior managers and employees and, to a lesser extent, regular newsletters. The use of multiple channels of communication was particularly marked in the union sector. However, the changing mixture still appeared to give employees in unionised workplaces a number of opportunities to be formally consulted by management, since the growth in new channels of communication was not confined to essentially 'top-down' ones.

In the non-union sector, there was virtually no shrinkage in the use of consultative committees, but these were always even less common in this sector. There was growth here in the use of regular (but usually infrequent) meetings between senior managers and the workforce; and a slight increase in the use of newsletters. However, the regular use of the orthodox chain of communication (from senior to junior managers to workers) was the only one of the six channels of communication we asked about which was used by the majority of non-union workplaces in both 1984 and 1990. Nor in the non-union sector was there a noticeable increase in the use of multiple channels of communication, as there was in the union sector. But perhaps of greatest importance was the fact that the methods of communication that were increasingly used in the non-union sector were the ones most clearly of a 'top-down' nature and did little to increase opportunities for employees to make a wider impact on the functioning of their workplace.

A further strand of our analysis of the use of management-employee communication channels was to focus on younger workplaces. Generally speaking there were few substantial differences between younger and older workplaces in the arrangements for communication. Younger workplaces as a whole were just as likely to use the management chain, consultative committees and newsletters as older workplaces were. They were marginally less likely to use suggestion schemes. But the two types of regular meeting between managers and the workforce were more commonly used in younger workplaces. Meetings between senior managers and the workforce occurred in 45 per cent of younger workplaces compared with 37 of those that existed prior to 1984; both new, original workplaces and movers showed this higher usage. Regular meetings between junior managers and their subordinates were particularly a feature of new, original workplaces; 56 per cent of them used them, compared with 40 per cent of movers and 43 per cent of older workplaces. Taking the six channels of communication covered by our discussion so far, the average number used in new workplaces was 2.4 in new workplaces, 2.2 in older workplaces and 2.1 in movers during the period 1984 to 1990. There thus seems to be a slight tendency for new workplaces to have more elaborate arrangements for communication between management and employees – especially given their smaller size and the general tendency for larger workplaces to have more elaborate arrangements. But the difference is hardly large enough to presage a major change in the way managers and employees communicate with each other.

However, there were more substantial signs of change when we examined the other methods of communication (besides the six methods discussed above) reported by management. As mentioned earlier, our question about methods of communication included items other than the above six in both surveys. In 1984 respondents were specifically asked about *'surveys or ballots of employees' views or opinions'*; they were then asked about any other methods used, some of which were subsequently coded as *'notice boards'*. In 1990 the procedure was the same, but the *'other answers'* were all recoded to specific categories. These included *'notice boards'*, but also some new items such as *'videos or films'*, *'other individual personal communications'* and *'other meetings'*. None or these separate items were reported by more than 4 per cent of respondents. Given the lack of similarly disaggregated responses from our 1984 survey it is difficult to draw any conclusions about the changing use of these methods. Clearly they were not widespread and the main channels of communication between management and employees were those covered by the items we specifically asked about. But we can make valid comparisons between the two surveys about the prevalence of surveys or ballots, notice boards and all other methods. The results are shown in Table 5.6.

Surveys or ballots of employees' views or opinions were the most common of the other methods of communication between management and employees in both surveys. The main characteristics associated with their use are shown in the table, but we also examined others. It was surprising, for example, that foreign-owned workplaces had much the same levels of use as comparable UK-owned private sector workplaces. Less of a surprise was that new workplaces were rather less likely to use them than older workplaces. So neither of these types of workplace appear to have been particularly innovative in terms of this method of communication and it would be unrealistic to expect any great increase in the use of it arising from the changing population of workplaces.

**Table 5.6  Other methods used by management to communicate with or consult employees, 1984 and 1990**

*Percentages*

|  | Surveys or ballots | Notice boards | All other methods | *Unweighted base* | *Weighted base* |
|---|---|---|---|---|---|
| **1984** | | | | | |
| All trading sector | 10 | 1 | 8 | *1385* | *1373* |
| | | | | | |
| **1990** | | | | | |
| All trading sector | 16 | 2 | 10 | *1510* | *1452* |
| Private manufacturing | 7 | 3 | 7 | *630* | *426* |
| Private services | 17 | 1 | 11 | *799* | *980* |
| Public sector | 80 | * | 8 | *81* | *46* |
| Size of enterprise | | | | | |
| 25-499 employees | 5 | 1 | 7 | *347* | *660*[1] |
| 500-4,999 | 9 | 1 | 4 | *207* | *144* |
| 5,000-49,999 | 20 | 1 | 14 | *255* | *185* |
| 50,000 or more | 49 | 5 | 16 | *287* | *216* |
| No information | 18 | 2 | 9 | *414* | *248* |
| Size of workplace | | | | | |
| 25-99 employees | 14 | 2 | 9 | *528* | *1136* |
| 100-499 employees | 21 | 3 | 11 | *555* | *288* |
| 500-999 | 32 | 2 | 8 | *194* | *19* |
| 1,000 or more | 38 | 3 | 16 | *233* | *8* |
| Union representation | | | | | |
| Unions recognised | 27 | 2 | 14 | *903* | *584* |
| No recognised unions | 9 | 2 | 6 | *607* | *868* |

Base: trading sector establishments

1.  See Note H.

But they did apparently become increasingly used during the course of the 1980s. The overall increase from 10 per cent of establishments in 1984 to 16 per cent in 1990 is substantial. But it was by no means evenly spread. The growth was very marked in state-owned enterprises, but it was also clearly apparent in other large, service sector organisations. As the table shows, surveys or ballots were very uncommon in smaller organisations, but widespread among establishments belonging to large enterprises. (Workplace size was a much weaker source of variation in this case than enterprise size). The much greater use of employee surveys in large enterprises seems only reasonable in view of the cost and professional expertise needed to organise them and the greater likelihood of large enterprises having the necessary resources, especially enterprises with a substantial head office personnel function. But there was also a noticeable difference in their use between the union and the non-union sector. Table 5.6 gives the overall difference; 27 per cent of unionised workplaces used them, compared with only 9 per cent of non-union workplaces. Even when we controlled for enterprise size in our analysis of the 1990 results, their greater use in the union sector was still apparent. Indeed, the growth between 1984 and 1990 in the use of surveys or ballots of employees' views or opinions was entirely confined to workplaces with union representation. As with our earlier analysis of meetings between management and employees, it seems reasonable to interpret this as an initiative by managements to increase direct communication with employees, without using trade unions as an intermediary. It would be wrong, however, to regard surveys or ballots as a replacement for consultative arrangements where employees have regular opportunities to raise issues of their choosing, rather than management's.

Earlier in this chapter we referred to the 'new union deals' that captured attention in the 1980s and to the use of formal consultative committees or councils in workplaces with a sole union agreement. Despite the popular stereotype, we found that these two features of management-employee relations were not strongly associated. Indeed, workplaces having both of those arrangements were extremely rare. But if workplaces with sole union representation were no more likely to have consultative committees or similar bodies than other single union workplaces, did they have a distinctive system of communication based upon other types of arrangement? The answer from our results in Table 5.7 seems to be that they did.

Workplaces with a sole union agreement were considerably more likely to use most of the eight specific methods of communication given in the table, according to our management respondents, than was the case for workplaces with a single union but no sole union agreement. The greater use of regular meetings between management and employees, of the conventional management chain of communication, of suggestion schemes, employee newsletters and of employee opinion surveys was substantial. So was the greater use of any of the other methods that respondents mentioned spontaneously such as videos and films.

**Table 5.7   Communication methods in single union establishments, 1990**

|  | Sole union agreement | No formal agreement |
|---|---|---|
|  |  | *Percentages* |
| Regular meetings with junior management | 57 | 44 |
| Regular meetings with senior management | 44 | 28 |
| Management chain of communication | 73 | 45 |
| Suggestion scheme | 41 | 18 |
| Regular newsletters | 54 | 38 |
| Functioning consultative committee | 17 | 14 |
| Surveys or ballots of employees' views | 23 | 9 |
| Noticeboards | 3 | 1 |
| All other methods | 29 | 16 |
|  |  | *Means* |
| Average number of first 6 methods | 2.9 | 1.9 |

Base:  trading sector establishments with a single recognised trade union

| | | |
|---|---|---|
| *Unweighted* | *136* | *124* |
| *Weighted* | *131* | *160* |

Workplaces with sole union agreements were much more likely to use multiple methods than other workplaces with a single recognised union: the average for the former was 2.9 compared with 1.9 for the latter. Moreover, the differences could not be explained away by the effects of workplace size. When we controlled for this in our analysis, workplaces with a sole union agreement remained distinctive in their wider range of methods of communication between management and the workforce, although they were no more likely to have a consultative committee or similar body. We showed in Chapter 4 that union representation in workplaces with a sole union agreement was more comprehensive in its coverage of the workforce and in some respects more vigorous. It would be consistent with that analysis to interpret some of the greater use of multiple methods of communication and consultation in such workplaces as a management response to, or anticipation of, trade union or employee demands for greater involvement.

## The substance of communication and consultation

The foregoing sections have been concerned with the structures and methods by which management and employees communicate with each other at the place of work. Our analysis showed some changes in the mixture of methods over time and highlighted the wider range of methods used in workplaces with union representation and, distinctively, those with formal, sole union agreements. We now examine whether there is any relationship between the methods of communication and the amount of information actually flowing between management and the workforce. Of course, our picture is a partial one. We did not ask questions about all the issues that might be relevant; we have no data from individual employees about what information they received from management; and our responses from employee representatives only come from trade union representatives.[15] Nevertheless we have a comprehensive set of responses from managers about the amount of information that they thought was given by management concerning a number of employee relations issues which are likely to be salient to all workplaces. Of the seven issues asked about in our 1990 survey we focus in the following analysis on three: 'staffing or manpower plans', 'major changes in working methods or work organisation' and 'the financial position of the establishment'.[16] The survey question asked, 'does management here give employees or their representatives information about the following items before the implementation of any changes in them?' Where the respondent answered affirmatively the interviewer asked, 'is that a lot of information or a little information?' Responses indicating that a lot of information was given by management to employees can be used as a crude indicator of the amount of information given. Naturally, as the earlier volume made clear, responses from worker representatives to similarly worded questions indicated rather lower amounts of information being given to employees.[17] But the pattern of responses was generally similar and the lack of worker representatives in the non-union sector pushes us in the direction of using the data from managers, which we have for the whole of our sample.

The analysis in the earlier volume indicated no dramatic change from 1984 to 1990 in the amount of information given by management to employees or their representatives. If anything there was a slight downward shift in the proportion of establishments where managers reported giving a good deal of information on several of the issues asked about, but most noticeably on staffing and manpower plans. Given the greater flow of

## Table 5.8   The amount of information given by management to employees or their representatives, by type of union representation, 1990

*Percentages*

| | All trading sector | No recognised union | Single recognised union | | Multiple recognised unions |
| | | | Sole union agreement | No formal agreement | |
|---|---|---|---|---|---|
| Proportion of workplaces where manager reported: | | | | | |
| Giving a lot of information on - | | | | | |
| Staffing or manpower plans | 26 | 20 | 39 | 23 | 35 |
| Working methods or work organisation | 63 | 59 | 75 | 51 | 75 |
| Financial position of workplace | 26 | 20 | 44 | 20 | 36 |
| Consulting employees or representatives about - | | | | | |
| Staffing or manpower plans | 38 | 31 | 46 | 27 | 60 |
| Working methods or work organisation | 68 | 63 | 82 | 57 | 80 |
| Base: trading sector establishments | | | | | |
| *Unweighted* | *1510* | *607* | *136* | *124* | *614* |
| *Weighted* | *1452* | *868* | *131* | *160* | *269* |

1.   See Note H.

information to employees in unionised workplaces, some of which might be attributed to legislative support,[18] that change was consistent with the contraction of the unionised sector over the period. In the trading sector of the economy, which is the focus of our attention in this volume, that analysis held true and needs no repetition here. We focus instead on the situation in 1990 among workplaces with different types of trade union representation to see whether the pattern of responses on the *methods* of communication was matched by a similar pattern on the *amount* of communication. The upper half of Table 5.8 gives the relevant results.

The pattern is highly consistent. For each of the three issues, managers in the non-union sector were less likely than managers in unionised workplaces to report that employees were given a lot of information. Within the unionised sector, information was more widely made available in workplaces with multiple recognised unions than in workplaces with a single union, part of this difference reflecting differences in the size of workplaces. However, workplaces with a sole union agreement were different from other single union workplaces. Those with sole union agreements reported information flows greater than in other single union workplaces (even when size was taken into account) and as great as in the generally much larger multi-union workplaces. The pattern did indeed bear a striking resemblance to the pattern for the methods of communication discussed earlier.

A similar result emerged from responses to a subsequent set of questions about the extent of employee consultation. The lower portion of Table 5.8 gives the results for two issues, 'staffing or manpower plans' and 'major changes in working methods or work organisation'. Again the lesser extent of consultation within the non-union sector is evident. And within the unionised sector, consultation is clearly more widespread within workplaces with a sole union agreement than in other single union workplaces.

Sole union agreements are thus associated with a greater number and variety of channels of communication between management and employees, although not a greater use of formal consultative committees or councils, and also with a greater flow of information to employees and more extensive consultation. To the extent that these are indicators of more effective representation of employees or of greater 'employee involvement', the single union agreement appears to be a distinctive and beneficial form of representation.

**Employee involvement through financial participation**

While part of the debate in the 1980s and early 1990s about employee involvement centred on the types of structure and practice that this chapter has so far been concerned with, another part focused upon arrangements that in one way or another gave employees a more direct financial stake in the success of their employing organisation than already existed through their basic wage or salary and through their prospects for continuing employment. Under the heading of 'employee financial participation' we consider here a variety of such arrangements ranging from direct payments or bonuses based upon the financial results of the employing unit to employee share-ownership schemes. We exclude arrangements such as individual or group-based payment by results and we exclude share or profits schemes that are fundamentally restricted to managerial employees or company directors. Our concern is with broadly-based schemes.

The present analysis has two main purposes. The first is to give a picture of the extent of employee financial participation schemes that supplements that already given in the earlier volume. The second is to see whether employee financial participation was complemented by the other arrangements for employee involvement discussed earlier in the chapter; in essence, did the two types of 'employee involvement' practice – financial and non-financial – go hand in hand or are they substitutes?

The questions on the various types of broadly-based financial participation scheme in the 1990 WIRS focused on five types of scheme:

- *establishment or organisation-wide payments or bonuses;*
- *profit related payments* or bonuses (including those covered by the 1987 Finance Act);
- *deferred profit sharing schemes,* where profits are put in a trust fund which acquires shares in the employing company for employees (sometimes under the 1978 Finance Act);
- *SAYE share option schemes,* where employees can buy their employer's shares from the proceeds of a Save As You Earn savings contract (sometimes under the 1980 Finance Act); and
- *other share ownership schemes.*

The first type of scheme was asked about during a sequence of questions, covering up to eight occupational groups, concerning various types of payment by results. This we defined as any method of payment where pay varies according the amount done or its value. Follow-up questions asked whether employees were paid on an establishment or organisational basis; it is positive responses to these follow-up questions that we have taken as indicating the presence of a broadly-based payment or bonus, based on the performance of the whole establishment or some larger organisational entity such as a division, company or group of companies. It is likely that many of these payments are infrequent or ad hoc, often very much at the discretion of management rather than dependent on the achievement of predefined targets. Nevertheless they still come within the scope of financial participation schemes. The four remaining types of scheme listed above were asked about separately, a little later in the interview. Respondents were asked whether the company owning their establishment operated any of the schemes listed on a card; the card defined the four schemes itemised above and also included 'discretionary or executive share option schemes' (excluded from our present analysis). [19]

Table 5.9 gives the overall extent of the five types of financial participation scheme under discussion.

Profit-related payments or bonuses were by far the most common type of scheme, being reported in 40 per cent of workplaces in the trading sector. The other type of cash-based scheme, establishment or enterprise-based payment by results, was reported in 7 per cent. Because of our separate and rather rudimentary questions on these two types of arrangement, these estimates may be imprecise. But given the quite different distribution among different types of organisation of the two schemes (discussed below) it is unlikely that any blurring of the two types is very substantial. Clearly profit-related payment or bonus schemes were a widespread phenomenon in British industry and commerce by 1990. As we showed in our earlier volume, they had grown dramatically since our 1984 survey, particularly in the retailing, financial services and engineering industries. Our panel data confirmed the spread of cash-based profit sharing to many workplaces that previously were not covered by them.

However, there are clearly limits to such growth. Not all organisations in the trading sector can readily distribute profits to employees, even if management decided that this was desirable. Three categories of ownership in Table 5.9 have an understandably lower incidence of cash-based profit-sharing because they include such cases: the public sector; foreign-owned companies; and trusts, charities and friendly societies (included in the category 'not limited company or PLC' in the table). It is also not surprising that smaller enterprises were substantially less likely to operate cash-based profit sharing: more of them are likely to be private companies with working proprietors and fewer of them are likely to have the organisational resources to operate such a scheme.

The other type of cash-based scheme, establishment or enterprise-based payment by results, was relatively common in only two types of organisation. In the public (trading) sector a quarter of establishments had such payments and among workplaces belonging to overseas companies

Table 5.9 Extent of employee financial participation schemes in industry and commerce, 1990, by type of enterprise

Percentages

| | Establishment or enterprise-wide bonus | Type of scheme: Profit-related pay or bonus | Deferred profit-sharing | SAYE share option | Other share ownership | Any of the 5 types | Un-weighted base | Weighted base |
|---|---|---|---|---|---|---|---|---|
| All trading sector | 7 | 40 | 9 | 24 | 7 | 55[1] | 1510 | 1452 |
| Ownership: | | | | | | | | |
| Private sector, all establishments | 7 | 41 | 9 | 25 | 7 | 56 | 1429 | 1406 |
| Limited company or PLC | 7 | 44 | 11 | 29 | 8 | 60 | 1301 | 1205[2] |
| Not limited company or PLC* | 6 | 26 | - | - | 2 | 28 | 128 | 200 |
| UK-owned | 6 | 42 | 10 | 26 | 7 | 56 | 1162 | 1250 |
| UK multinational | 7 | 53 | 20 | 58 | 13 | 79 | 640 | 451 |
| Foreign-owned | 17 | 30 | 1 | 4 | 7 | 45 | 219 | 137 |
| Public sector | 25 | 3 | - | - | - | 28 | 81 | 46 |
| Size of enterprise in UK | | | | | | | | |
| Less than 500 employees | 4 | 30 | 1 | 1 | 2 | 33 | 347 | 660 |
| 500-4,999 | 6 | 46 | 6 | 26 | 3 | 60 | 207 | 144 |
| 5,000-49,999 | 14 | 47 | 17 | 44 | 12 | 76 | 255 | 185 |
| 50,000 or more | 7 | 55 | 34 | 70 | 20 | 84 | 287 | 216 |
| No information | 11 | 47 | 3 | 28 | 7 | 69 | 414 | 248 |

Base: trading sector establishments

* Includes: companies limited by guarantee, trusts, friendly societies, charities, cooperatives, partnerships and self-proprietorships.
1. See Note F.
2. See Note H.

the proportion was nearly a fifth. Elsewhere they were reported in less than a tenth of workplaces. Taking the two types of cash-based scheme together, foreign-owned workplaces were almost as likely to make either type of payment to employees as workplaces owned by British companies, the proportion being just under one half in both cases.

The other broad type of financial participation arrangement, employee share ownership, was much less common than profit sharing or profit-related payments. The most common of the three schemes identified in our questioning was the SAYE share option, reported in 24 per cent of establishments. Deferred profit-sharing and other types of employee share ownership were reported in 9 per cent and 7 per cent of workplaces respectively. All these schemes were very much more common in larger enterprises than in smaller ones. UK-based multi-national companies were particularly likely to operate them. The finance sector and the distribution sector stood out as the ones where employees in most workplaces were covered by such schemes.

A broad measure of the existence of some form of financial participation arrangement is whether employees were affected by, or had access to, any of the five types of scheme discussed above. Using this measure, 55 per cent of workplaces and 62 per cent of employees in industry and commerce and covered by our 1990 survey were affected or potentially affected by these arrangements. As Table 5.10 indicates, white-collar employees were those most likely to benefit; where white-collar (non-manual) employees formed a clear majority of the workforce the incidence of any scheme – and of each of the five individual schemes – was substantially greater than in workplaces where manual workers formed the majority.

There was little difference in the extent of financial participation arrangements between unionised and non-union workplaces. Overall, 57 per cent of workplaces with recognised trade unions had a scheme compared with 54 per cent of non-union workplaces. Moreover, when only white-collar workers were considered, schemes were more common where there was union representation; 64 per cent of workplaces with recognised unions for non-manual employees had a scheme, compared with 51 per cent of cases where non-manual workers had no union representation. The difference was confined to smaller enterprises – those with under 5,000 employees. Here the greater incidence of financial participation in unionised workplaces was largely accounted for by just two types of scheme: deferred profit-sharing and SAYE share option schemes, both of which were very much more common in workplaces with recognised non-manual unions. It seems likely that favourable approaches to such

**Table 5.10 Extent of employee financial participation schemes in industry and commerce, 1990, by workforce composition and trade union representation**

Percentages

| | Establishment or enterprise-wide bonus | Type of scheme: | | | Other share ownership | Any of the 5 types | Un-weighted base | Weighted base |
| --- | --- | --- | --- | --- | --- | --- | --- | --- |
| | | Profit-related pay or bonus | Deferred profit-sharing | SAYE share option | | | | |
| **Proportion of employees who were manual:** | | | | | | | | |
| More than 70% | 5 | 30 | 5 | 21 | 6 | 46[1] | 648 | 648 |
| Between 31% and 70% | 9 | 40 | 5 | 18 | 3 | 55 | 410 | 372 |
| Between 0% and 30% | 9 | 56 | 19 | 32 | 11 | 68 | 452 | 431 |
| **Union representation (all employees)** | | | | | | | | |
| No union recognition | 6 | 42 | 4 | 16 | 6 | 54 | 607 | 868 |
| Unions recognised | 9 | 37 | 16 | 36 | 8 | 57 | 903 | 584 |
| Single recognised union | 8 | 35 | 13 | 30 | 4 | 51 | 289 | 315 |
| Sole union agreement | 15 | 53 | 22 | 38 | 3 | 69 | 136 | 131 |
| Single union, no agreement | 3 | 22 | 6 | 22 | 6 | 38 | 124 | 160 |
| Multiple recognised unions | 10 | 39 | 20 | 43 | 12 | 63 | 614 | 269 |
| **Union representation for white-collar employees** | | | | | | | | |
| No union recognised | 6 | 39 | 4 | 17 | 6 | 51 | 782 | 1048 |
| Unions recognised | 10 | 43 | 22 | 41 | 10 | 64 | 727 | 400 |

Base: trading sector establishments

1. See Note F.

schemes by some white-collar unions, as well as management preferences, account for their greater prevalence here than in sectors dominated by blue-collar unions.

A further link with union representation, also shown in Table 5.10, is with the number of unions recognised by management. Workplaces with multiple unions were rather more likely to have financial participation schemes than those with a single union, largely because of the association with enterprise size. However, among workplaces with a single recognised union, those with a sole union agreement were nearly twice as likely to have a financial participation scheme as those without a sole union agreement. This again casts doubt on the stereotype of single union representation that emerged in the late 1980s. Financial participation schemes were not part of the stereotypical single union deal; indeed, recent detailed studies of single-union deals make no mention of profit-sharing or employee share ownership as one of the mechanisms for enhancing employee cooperation and commitment that the deals were designed to foster.[20] Yet nearly 70 per cent of workplaces in 1990 that had a sole union agreement also had one of these forms of financial participation. This contrasts with our earlier finding that workplaces with sole union agreements were no more likely that other workplaces to have a consultative committee or company council, one of the key features of the typical 'single union deal'. The type of arrangement instituted by management to engender employee commitment and cooperation in situations where sole union representation had been negotiated, appears from our results to have been quite different from what was concluded by looking at the specific cases that constituted the package deals of the 1980s. Sole union agreements were more associated with financial participation schemes than with non-financial employee-involvement mechanisms.

Turning back to the general picture in the trading sector as a whole, we are now able to see the extent to which financial and non-financial employee involvement arrangements coincided. For this we use the broadest measure of the two types of arrangement possible with our survey data. For financial participation we take the existence of any of the five types of profit-sharing or employee share-ownership scheme discussed above: 55 per cent of establishments had such a scheme. As our measure of the existence of any non-financial arrangement that might encourage employee commitment we take the existence of any of the six methods of communication between management and the workforce discussed in the earlier section of this chapter – briefing groups, suggestion schemes, newsletters, consultative committees and even systematic use of the management chain of communication. Altogether 84 per cent of establishments used at least one of these arrangements as a matter of policy and practice. The two types of arrangement were strongly associated. One half (49 per cent) of our sample had both a financial and non-financial mechanism for engendering employee commitment. In these cases it would be reasonable to infer that the financial mechanisms that corporate personnel had put in place to engender employee commitment were reinforced by local, non-financial communication structures with somewhat similar goals. On the other hand, 11 per cent of cases had neither type of mechanism. That is to say they had none of the five forms of financial participation discussed above nor did they have any of the six methods of communication or consultation discussed earlier. The size of this minority must be a disappointment to those who argue that management should make at least some attempt to communicate regularly with employees, give them an opportunity to participate in their work situation or participate financially other than through the wage nexus.

It should be no surprise that the workplaces with none of these arrangements were almost exclusively non-union and that most of them were small firms.

### 'Single status' employment

The final element of the 'new industrial relations' that we examine in this chapter is the degree to which employees were treated in a unified way, rather than under the highly differentiated arrangements that accorded inferior treatment to 'workers' as compared with 'staff' in much of traditional industry. Moves towards 'single status', often termed 'harmonisation', have been regarded by many commentators as one of the more progressive developments in British industry and British industrial relations during the last two decades. Single status was one of the key elements of 'human resource management'. According to some reports, it was particularly associated with newly-established Japanese manufacturing plants, although it was by no means confined to them.[21] It featured in most of the 'single union agreements' as another of the means of encouraging employee commitment and flexibility.[22]

Employees are, of course, treated differently in myriad ways. Many of the distinctions would be too subtle to be captured by standardised interviews in a large-scale survey covering all types of workplace; on the other hand, a broad question about the existence or absence of single status at a workplace would be liable to miss important distinctions in the treatment of different categories of worker and hence greatly overstate the phenomenon. Instead, our approach is to focus on two of the most important aspects of the employment relationship for which we do have relevant information in the WIRS series: these are, first, on methods of payment and control and, secondly, on the distribution of fringe benefits. These are both areas where we have data that enable us to determine whether manual and non-manual employees were treated in a broadly similar manner. Naturally our analysis is confined to workplaces employing both manual and non-manual workers. Some of the questions permit finer distinctions to be made, for example between different grades of non-manual worker, but for simplicity and comparability across the various methods of payment and fringe benefit discussed in this analysis the distinction between manual and non-manual employees is sufficient.

The first two questions considered here are those that capture the broad distinction between a wage and a salary. The first asked how frequently most manual employees were paid. The second asked whether they were paid in cash, by cheque or by direct transfer to a bank or similar account. Comparable questions were asked about non-manual employees. Similar questions in the 1980 WIRS enable us to document the dramatic change in these two aspects of wage and salary payment during the 1980s. We mention this briefly before concentrating on the differential treatment of the two categories of employee, which is relevant to the discussion of single status.

In 1980 most manual workers were paid in cash in 80 per cent of workplaces in the trading sector. By 1990 this proportion dropped to 35 per cent. For non-manual workers the 1980 figure was 34 per cent and by 1990 this was down to 12 per cent. Thus both broad groups of employees experienced a very substantial move towards cashless pay, a move no doubt influenced by the declining cost and increased used of computerised payroll systems, the spread of bank accounts and other factors. By 1990 the great majority of manual workers were treated as 'staff' in this one respect, the form in which they received their pay.

There were also shifts towards 'staff conditions' in terms of the frequency of payment. In 1980 most manual workers were paid weekly (or fortnightly) in 91 per cent of establishments in industry and commerce. By 1990 the comparable figure was 74 per cent. For non-manual employees the respective figures were 39 and 27 per cent. So monthly payment, the typical method for white-collar staff, became increasingly common for manual workers; but it remained a minority practice for them, no doubt in many cases a reflection of their dislike of infrequent pay-packets or the inappropriateness of monthly pay when their period of notice was shorter than this.

The above results indicate very substantial movement towards what were traditionally regarded as typical 'staff' conditions of employment. The

**Table 5.11 Indicators of 'single status' with respect to manual and non-manual workers, 1980 and 1990**

*Percentages*

|  | 1980 | 1990 |
|---|---|---|
| Proportion of establishments where most manual workers and most non-manual workers were treated similarly: | | |
| Same frequency of payment (weekly or 2-weekly; monthly) | 45 | 51 |
| Same method of payment (cash; cheque; direct transfer) | 47 | 73 |
| Same recording of attendance (clocking; other method; no recording) | 48 | 52 |
| Base: trading sector establishments employing both manual and non-manual workers and supplying relevant information | | |
| *Unweighted* | *1382* | *1345* |
| *Weighted* | *1314* | *1237* |

movement was greater for manual workers, but was also apparent for non-manuals. But was there a shift *within workplaces* towards equality of treatment? Table 5.11 shows the results from the 1980 and 1990 WIRS surveys that come from identifying workplaces where the majority of manual workers and the majority of non-manual workers were treated in the same way with regard to these two aspects of wage or salary payment. Both measures show a move towards single status. The increase was a modest one with respect to the frequency of payment, but quite marked with respect to the method of payment.

In 1990 roughly a half of establishments paid the majority of their manual and the majority of their white-collar employees at the same interval. However, there were as many cases where the period was weekly as where it was monthly or 4-weekly. So the equality of treatment should not be taken as an indication that manual employees were being treated as salaried workers. In half of the cases where there was equality, white-collar workers were being treated as wage-earners in respect of the frequency of their payment.

In 1990, too, nearly three quarters of establishments paid most manual and most non-manual employees by the same method. But here there was a predominance of the typically 'staff' method of payment. Over 80 per cent of cases were ones where the majority of both groups of employee received 'cashless pay', 90 per cent of them by direct transfer to a bank or building society account.

Our third, and perhaps more telling, indicator of 'single status' employment conditions concerned the method of recording employees' attendance. The stereotype that our 1980 survey confirmed in manufacturing industry was that manual workers were required to clock in and out at the start and finish of their working day whereas white-collar staff did not have their starting and finishing times formally recorded at all. That was still the picture in 1990 in manufacturing. In service industries the differences between the two groups of employee were less marked and other methods of recording starting and finishing times were as common as clocking in and out.[23] Our focus here is on the degree of equality of treatment within workplaces and the last line in Table 5.11 shows that this may have increased a little between 1980 and 1990.[24] Even so, only a half (52 per cent) of all workplaces in industry and commerce in 1990 treated the majority of their manual and non-manual workers alike with respect to recording their starting and finishing times. Just under half of these cases were ones where both manuals and non-manuals did not have their hours of work formally recorded, the 'high-trust' arrangement associated with staff or salaried work and advocated by the proponents of 'human resource management'.

We are now in a position to use these three indicators of 'single-status' employment conditions to examine the types of workplace in which it was most common and thus to see whether it coincided with other new, or supposedly new, industrial relations practices. We do this by combining the three aspects and hence identifying workplaces where, on all of the three indicators, most manual and most non-manual employees worked under the same arrangement. Altogether 33 per cent of workplaces in industry and commerce in 1990 fitted this loose definition of 'single status'.

The least likely types of workplace to have single status were those belonging to the state-owned industries and those in manufacturing industry (Table 5.12). Only 5 per cent of state-owned trading sector establishments had single status, largely because of their practice of paying manual workers on a weekly basis and white-collar workers monthly. The overall figure for manufacturing was 15 per cent of plants with single status, compared with 43 per cent in service industries. Other differences followed from this clear distinction between manufacturing and services. Single status was considerably more common where the workforce was predominantly female and predominantly white-collar (but it should be remembered that we are considering workplaces that do employ some manual workers). The

**Table 5.12 The extent of three features of common conditions of employment
for manual and non-manual employees, 1990**

*Percentages*

| | | Unweighted base | Weighted base |
|---|---|---|---|
| Proportion of workplaces where each of three common conditions of employment* were reported: | | | |
| All trading sector | 33 | *1342* | *1238* |
| Public sector | 5 | *75* | *42* |
| Private sector | 34 | *1267* | *1196* |
| Manufacturing | 15 | *621* | *418* |
| Services | 43 | *721* | *820* |
| Private sector only: | | | |
| UK-owned | 34 | *1024*[1] | *1063* |
| Foreign-owned | 37 | *197* | *122* |
| Older workplaces | 34 | *1065* | *938* |
| Younger workplaces | 37 | *202* | *258* |
| Unions recognised | 32 | *754* | *443* |
| No recognised unions | 36 | *513* | *753* |
| Recognised union(s) with both non-manual and manual members | 45 | *429* | *198* |
| Member of employers' association | 23 | *205* | *175* |

Base:  trading sector establishments with both manual and non-manual workers

---

\*    The three conditions of employment were: frequency of pay; method of payment; and recording of hours worked.

1.    See Note G.

financial services sector was the industry with the highest proportion of workplaces with single status, but even here the figure was only 60 per cent.

Because the state sector was so obviously different in its lack of single status arrangements we now focus on the picture within the private sector. The remainder of Table 5.12 indicates that a number of pieces of conventional wisdom about the extent of single status are hardly sustainable on the basis of our evidence.

First of all, the association between foreign ownership and single status is called into question. The literature on 'japanisation' and the specific studies of single union agreements, most of which were with overseas companies, indicated that single status conditions were a distinctive feature of foreign-owned workplaces. Our representative national sample shows that this was hardly the case. The difference in 1990 between foreign-owned and British-owned workplaces (37 per cent compared with 34 per cent) was insignificant. Moreover, when we compared foreign and British-owned establishments within the service sector and, separately, within manufacturing there was no marked tendency for single status to be associated with foreign ownership. And when we confined our comparisons within manufacturing industry to manufacturing plants (thus excluding the head offices of manufacturing firms) British owned plants were no less likely to have single status than foreign-owned plants. In both cases the proportion having single status conditions was around 15 per cent.

Secondly, there was no clear tendency for younger workplaces to have single status conditions. In the private sector 37 per cent of workplaces established in 1984 or later had single status, compared with 34 per cent of older workplaces. Original new workplaces were less likely to have it than movers; indeed, the slightly higher rate for younger workplaces overall was attributable to service sector establishments that had moved within the last six years. The view that greenfield sites are especially likely to adopt single status arrangements is not borne out by our results.

Thirdly, the idea that single status arrangements are the preserve of non-union firms or of those with single-union agreements receives little or no support. Workplaces without recognised unions were marginally more likely to have single status (36 per cent compared with 32 per cent for those with recognised unions), but this was largely because there were more non-union establishments in the services sector where single status was more common; looking at manufacturing and services separately revealed no difference between union and non-union establishments. Workplaces with sole union agreements were indistinguishable from other unionised workplaces.

There was, however, one feature of trade union organisation that did appear to be associated with single status arrangements. Where a recognised union or unions represented both manual and non-manual workers the extent of single status arrangements was substantially greater. In fact, 45 per cent of workplaces with such 'mixed' unions had single status. The difference was particularly marked in the service sector, where 62 per cent of cases with recognised unions covering both groups of employee had the arrangement. This result suggests that unions which recruit and represent a broad range of occupations at workplace level either acquiesce more readily to single status arrangements or positively encourage them. If this interpretation is accepted then at least one part of the stereotype of 'progressive' trade unionism received some empirical support.

Within the unionised sector, however, the clearest source of variation in the extent of single status was the structure of pay determination. Single status was much less common in workplaces where pay was the subject of multi-employer agreements. Thus only 23 per cent of establishments that were members of an employers' association had single status compared with 36 per cent of non-members. But single status was also uncommon where pay negotiations were at plant level. It was most prevalent where there was enterprise level bargaining over pay, even if trade unions representing manual and non-manual employees negotiated separately. It therefore seems that, far from single union representation being most conducive to single status arrangements, it is enterprise bargaining that provides the most fertile conditions for it, provided that both major groups of employee are represented by recognised unions.

It would be too simple, however, to base such conclusions on the narrow conception of 'single status' that we have used so far. Methods of wage or salary payment and the recording of hours worked are only a part of the range of employment conditions which need to be harmonised before we can reasonably classify an establishment as having single status arrangements. The present study does not aspire to be comprehensive in this respect since to do so would have required a much greater range of questioning on this one subject than was possible within the confines of a broadly-based survey like WIRS. However, we can add substantially to the picture of 'single status' arrangements by using the results of some simple questions on the extent of fringe benefit provision, asked for the first time in the 1990 survey with this purpose in mind. To make the results comparable in nature to those discussed above on payment methods and the recording of hours worked, we maintain the simple distinction between manual and non-manual employees and confine our attention to workplaces where both types were employed.[25]

The four fringe benefits asked about were all ones on which manual and white-collar workers were treated similarly in the majority of workplaces. In 94 per cent of workplaces both groups of workers had free or subsidised meals or else neither group did. Sick pay above the statutory requirements was available to both or neither groups in 79 per cent of workplaces. Occupational pensions were similarly available in 76 per cent or workplaces. A standard working week of less than 36 hours was the rule for either both groups or neither group in 82 per cent. Taking the four fringe benefits together, 54 per cent of workplaces in industry and commerce that employed both manual and non-manual employees had the same basic provision (or lack of provision) on all these benefits for both groups of worker.

**Table 5.13 The extent of equal provision of (a) four fringe benefits and (b) seven indicators of 'single status' for manual and non-manual workers, 1990**

*Percentages*

| | Four fringe benefits | Seven 'single status' indicators | Unweighted base | Weighted base |
|---|---|---|---|---|
| Proportion of establishments where manual and non-manual employees received broadly equal conditions: | | | | |
| All trading sector | 54 | 19 | *1224* | *999* |
| Public sector | 86 | 7 | *61* | *15* |
| Private sector | 54 | 19 | *1163* | *984* |
| Manufacturing | 52 | 7 | *603* | *375* |
| Services | 55 | 27 | *621* | *624* |
| Private sector only: | | | | |
| UK-owned | 53 | 19 | *929*[1] | *864* |
| Foreign-owned | 56 | 23 | *192* | *113* |
| Older workplaces | 53 | 19 | *991* | *770* |
| Younger workplaces | 54 | 20 | *172* | *214* |
| Unions recognised | 57 | 18 | *710* | *367* |
| No recognised unions | 51 | 20 | *453* | *616* |
| Recognised union(s) with both non-manual and manual members | 68 | 27 | *402* | *163* |
| Member of employers' association | 43 | 5 | *198* | *159* |

Base: trading sector establishments employing at least 5 manual and at least 5 non-manual employees

1. See Note G.

Table 5.13 shows how this indicator of the equality of treatment regarding fringe benefits varied by a number of establishment characteristics. As with the previous indicator of 'single status' treatment, the state-owned enterprises stood out as different, but this time by their much greater equality of provision: 86 per cent of state-owned workplaces provided similar benefits to manual and non-manual employees. Again in contrast to the previous indicator, manufacturing and service industries were very similar. In terms of industries, energy and water supply (largely ex-public sector) had the highest level of equality regarding fringe benefits (83 per cent); the construction industry had the lowest (18 per cent). There were rather weak associations with workforce composition. Equality was somewhat more prevalent in workplaces where men predominated and where most employees were in white-collar occupations.

To maintain comparability with the foregoing discussion of single-status employment conditions and again because the public sector was distinctive, the remainder of our analysis of fringe-benefit equality is based upon private sector workplaces. The lower half of Table 5.13 shows that, in this respect too, much conventional wisdom about the incidence of single status is misplaced.

First, the difference between foreign-owned and UK owned workplaces (56 per cent compared with 53 per cent) was again insignificant. Moreover, there were no clear differences between the two types of workplace when we examined manufacturing and service sectors separately. It was certainly not the case, as was widely believed in the 1980s, that foreign-owned plants were much more likely to have universally available fringe benefits than their indigenously-owned counterparts.

Nor were new workplaces more progressive in this respect. The proportions of older and younger workplaces (using 1984 as the dividing line) were indistinguishable and within the category of 'younger workplaces', original new workplaces and movers were also the same. The expectation that greenfield sites typically had single status fringe benefits whereas older workplaces had different provisions for manual workers and staff was not borne out by the survey data.

Thirdly, there was no general tendency for non-union firms to provide single-status fringe benefits; unionised firms were just as likely to. Within the unionised sector it was multi-union workplaces where single status arrangements were most common: 74 per cent of them had single status fringe benefits compared with only 45 per cent where there was a single recognised union. Single union workplaces with a sole union agreement were no different from other single union workplaces. But, as with our earlier indicator of single-status conditions, workplaces with a union representing both manual and non-manual employees were more likely to have broadly equal provision. And it was most likely where pay was negotiated at enterprise level, especially where negotiations covered both groups of employee.

Our final look at the issue of single status combines the two separate aspects of it discussed so far. We now take our indicator of whether a workplace with both manual and non-manual employees has single status employment conditions as whether it makes broadly equal provision on each of the seven measures: frequency of payment, method of payment, recording of hours, provision of meals, sick pay, pensions and the length of the standard working week. In all, 19 per cent of workplaces had this degree of equality of treatment of its manual and white-collar employees (Table 5.13). It was uncommon in manufacturing industry and in small, single-plant firms. Within the unionised sector it was least likely where there was multi-employer bargaining over pay or there was plant-level bargaining over pay, especially when this involved only one section of the workforce. It was not more common in workplaces with sole union agreements; the proportion for workplaces that had such agreements was again 19 per cent. In fact, single status arrangements seem to have much more commonly achieved where the structure of employee representation was more complex but provided opportunities for comparison and collaboration since it involved dealing with a single employer. Alternatively, trade unions with a broad catchment involving both manual and white-collar employees at the same workplace were also associated with the presence of single-status arrangements.

Single status, then, was another feature of industrial relations in Britain which was hardly the preserve of the new-style, single union deals of the 1980s. Moreover, workplaces that had just two of the features of 'new-style agreements', single status and a consultative committee or council, amounted to less than 4 per cent of our sample. Nor was single status strongly associated with the manifestations of 'human resource management' that the 1990 WIRS set out to measure. Only a fifth of the workplaces that reported having any of the six methods of communication between management and employees that we discussed earlier in this chapter also had single status according to the seven-item measure used above. Given that our measures of single status err on the side of being generous, and that our measure of the existence of direct communication channels between management and employees includes cases that merely have a regular management newsletter or a suggestion scheme, the extent of serious human resource management practices cannot be great. Indeed, if we take these two broad indicators of progressive management[26] – single status and at least one formal method of management-employee communication – there were nearly as many cases in our sample that had *neither* of these features (16 per cent of the total sample) as there were that had *both* (18 per cent). Judged by these two rather meagre yardsticks of progressive management practice, British industry and commerce still has substantial areas of potential for development.

## Notes and references

1. Industrial Relations Services, 'Single-union deals survey: 2', *Employment Trends,* No.529, p.6, 1993.

2. Neil Millward, David Smart, Mark Stevens and W.R. Hawes, *Workplace Industrial Relations in Transition: the ED/ESRC/PSI/ACAS Surveys,* Dartmouth Publishing, Aldershot, 1992, p.153.

3. In each of the WIRS surveys the question excluded single-issue committees such as those dealing only with health and safety matters, or welfare or recreational facilities. Negotiating committees, covered in earlier questioning, were also excluded.

4. This criterion was derived from an open question, 'What would you say was the most important matter discussed by this committee in the last 12 months?'. Responses were coded to a frame of some 25 substantive codes; those coded as 'Nothing important discussed' are the ones excluded from our current definition of a functioning committee.

5. The unweighted base for non-union closures is only 33 cases, so the figure is subject to a substantial margin of error.

6. Millward et al. (1992) pp.157-9.

7. Millward et al. (1992) p.159.

8. See J. MacInnes (1985) 'Conjuring up consultation: the role and extent of joint consultation in post-war private manufacturing', *British Journal of Industrial Relations,* July, pp.93-113; P. Bassett (1987), 'Consultation and the Right to Manage, 1980-1984', *British Journal of Industrial Relations,* July, pp.283-286.

9. Both the 1984 and 1990 surveys included 'Surveys or ballots of employees' views or opinions' and 'other answers'. These are excluded from the current analysis because there was no specification of how frequent they should be before the item was endorsed; it is unlikely that they are a regular occurrence in many cases. The 1990 question also included an item, 'Regular meetings among work-groups or teams at least once a month to discuss aspects of their performance, such as "quality circles" and other problem-solving groups'. Such meetings do not contain the essential element of worker-management communication that is our present concern. They are discussed in a later section of the chapter.

10. Rather more of our respondents in 1990 than in 1984 were based at higher-level or head offices (14 compared with 10 per cent) and this may have affected the comparisons. Higher-level respondents were considerably more likely to report some of the communication channels covered in the following discussion, particularly suggestion schemes and newsletters. To the extent that some of this might be over-reporting, the 1990 figures might be slight overestimates. The changes discussed at some length in the text are the least affected by this consideration.

11. Readers of the earlier volume may wish to note that a computational error led to incorrect figures for the overall extent of methods of communication in 1990 in Table 5.5. The 'all establishments' figures for 1990 shown in the bottom two substantive rows should read 84 (not 86) and 86 (not 87) per cent respectively. The change from 86 to 84 per cent between 1984 and 1990 does not quite reach the

# 6 Summary and conclusions

The transformation that has taken place in Britain's industrial relations since 1979 is now so much a part of conventional wisdom that further analysis of it may seem unnecessary. Few will doubt that trade unionism has been in retreat and that in many sectors of employment management has 'regained the right to manage'. So radical has been the change in the period since 1979 that industrial relations scholars have appeared to many people to be an endangered species, rather like the institutions that many of them study. If we truly have witnessed 'the end of institutional industrial relations', as one scholar poignantly entitled a recent article,[1] what more is there to say on the subject?

Of the many reasons that could be advanced for further analysis of the relationships between management and employees in Britain, the following must surely have some force. First, employee relations matter. They matter not only to those directly involved at the place of work, but they affect the whole of society and the national economy. Good employee relations make work more agreeable for workers and managers. Good relationships at work benefit social relations outside work – in the family and the wider community. They might even make work more intrinsically interesting, more productive or of better quality. In turn such benefits might lead to a more competitive economy with more investment, more jobs or higher incomes from employment. Secondly, how employee relations in Britain should be organised is a matter of continuing, lively debate, not only between the political parties but amongst managers in their professional bodies, amongst trade unionists, between various pressure groups, commentators and opinion formers. Those who argue for change, or who challenge or defend recent developments, may find value in more detailed, systematic information about how employee relations are actually organised and how they have changed in recent times. Thirdly, greater understanding of the sources of change may provide pointers to how further changes may be encouraged or undesirable trends arrested.

These, and many other, reasons for a continuing interest in employee relations at the place of work provide the motivation for the current inquiry. There is, of course, a continuing stream of information about current developments in the specialist press and through other communications media. So what is distinctive about the analysis that has been presented in this volume? Here again there are several strands to the response.

In the first place, the survey series on which the analysis has been based still represents the most comprehensive and up-to-date national source of systematic information on employee relations at the place of work. The Workplace Industrial Relations Surveys (WIRS) are unrivalled in terms of the representativeness of the information they provide and the coverage of the types of workplace that they include: large and small, public and private, manufacturing and services. The ability to make direct comparisons through time, starting with the first, benchmark survey in 1980, is a unique strength in this field of inquiry. In this respect, British industrial relations scholars and commentators are in a uniquely favourable position.

Secondly, the analysis in this volume has taken as its starting point the initial report[2] on the most recent survey and used the complete range of information from the WIRS series, either to address questions in greater depth or to address new questions. Thus we have examined in greater detail the decline of the institutions of collective bargaining that was one of the main features of the 1980s. We have looked further at the causes of that decline and at the changing nature of the remaining unionised sector. We have looked for 'the new industrial relations' of the single union deals that became such a talking point during the decade. And we have examined a number of features of employee relations in the growing non-union sector, including practices associated with the 'human resource management' movement.

Thirdly, the analysis has been distinctive in that it has drawn more widely from the resources of Workplace Industrial Relations Survey series than both the initial volume on the 1990 survey, *Workplace Industrial Relations in Transition*, and the more focused analyses of the survey that have emerged since the data became available for other researchers and scholars to use.[3] As we explained in Chapter 1, besides the main 1990 cross-sectional survey data, we have deployed three additional datasets: the supplementary sample of newer workplaces, established from 1987 onwards, and interviewed at in 1990 and early 1991; the sample of workplaces that had closed down between 1984 and 1990, but for which we had full information in 1984; and the panel sample of enduring workplaces, interviewed in both 1984 and 1990. Clearly we had the fullest information for the period 1984 to 1990 and this has been the focus of the analysis. The two panel samples (closures and enduring workplaces) were restricted to industry and commerce (the trading sector). In order to maintain coherence, this restriction was imposed upon all the analysis presented in the volume. The excluded sector, non-trading public services, is the subject of separate, ongoing research.

Fourthly, we have made more use of a number of new questions in the latest survey. One particularly important question was about the age of workplaces, which had only been asked in a very rudimentary manner in earlier surveys. This, together with the supplementary sample of the newest workplaces, enabled us to get a clearer idea of how changes in the population of workplaces was affecting the overall picture. Other new questions were aimed at measuring the extent of what were thought to be relatively new practices, such as 'pendulum arbitration' and 'team briefing'. In combination these new sources of information were designed to enhance our knowledge of the way industrial relations and, more generally, employee relations practices were changing.

## The retreat of traditional industrial relations

It may seem perverse to have started an inquiry about new forms of industrial relations by focusing on the traditional institutions of collective bargaining. The reasons for this were twofold. First, some of the newer practices such as single union agreements were variants of the established institutions and could be sensibly discussed only within that context. Secondly, there was much debate about the compatibility of many of the newer practices with trade union representation and traditional collective bargaining. It seemed sensible to discuss the latter as a backdrop to the former. This was the subject of Chapter 2.

Focusing on the period 1984 to 1990 and the trading sector of the economy, the decline in the collective representation of employees by recognised trade unions was stark and incontrovertible. The number of workplaces with recognised unions fell from 52 to 40 per cent in the six year period. The number of employees in such workplaces fell from 58 to 43 per cent.

Derecognition – a term almost unheard of in the early 1980s – accounted for a significant part of this decline. Our panel sample of workplaces with 25 employees in 1984 and 1990 revealed that union recognition had been withdrawn at 9 per cent of workplaces during the six-year period. Nearly a fifth of panel workplaces that reported recognised unions in 1984 had no recognised unions in 1990.[4] Changes in the opposite direction were far less numerous.

A second type of change, from full recognition to partial recognition, was found to be uncommon. When managements withdrew trade union recognition they did so comprehensively.

Given the lack of legal underpinning to trade union recognition since 1980, the continuance of recognition in the majority of cases already having it required an explanation. Managers in the majority of workplaces with recognised unions reported that any decision to derecognise the unions would be made by senior management above the level of the workplace, generally at the enterprise's headquarters. This tendency was stronger where pay was negotiated on a company or enterprise-wide basis. So much of the continuing recognition of unions could be attributed to a desire on the part of management to maintain existing centralised arrangements for the determination of pay. Only if union support dwindled substantially across entire companies or enterprises does it seem likely that wholesale derecognition would become a likely prospect.

The other main source of change behind the decline in trade union recognition was the changing population of workplaces. We were able to separate this into two distinct elements. One of these proved to be insignificant: workplaces that closed down in the period 1984 to 1990 were no more likely to have recognised trade unions than the generality of workplaces. If plant closures had been the only source of change in the extent of union recognition then the overall figure would have increased, not declined by nearly a quarter. The second element proved to be a major source of change. This was the substantially lower likelihood of newer establishments recognising unions – around 30 per cent of newer workplaces did so compared with 40 per cent of all workplaces in 1990. Many of the characteristics of newer workplaces predisposed them towards non-union status; they were smaller, mostly in service industries, employed fewer skilled manual workers and many more part-timers. But by doing a similar analysis of our original 1980 survey we showed that the tendency for younger workplaces to have lower rates of recognition was greater in the 1980s than in the previous decade. The drop in the rate of new recognition in the 1980s compared with the 1970s was especially marked in manufacturing industry. However, it was by no means confined to manufacturing, which in any case only accounted for a small proportion of new workplaces in the 1980s. Hence we concluded that the origins of the change were general and pervasive. Prime candidates appeared to be the removal of the statutory support for union recognition and the decline in the presumption by managements and the state in favour of collective bargaining between trade unions and employers.

A final twist to the story on compositional change is that the rate of turnover among establishments was higher in the 1980s than earlier. New establishments were being created at a faster rate which, with their lower rate of recognition, accentuated the decline in the overall extent of recognition.

## Single union representation

Against this backdrop of retreat for the trade unions, new workplaces were to become, in the 1980s, the seedbed for what many trade unionists hoped would be a revival of trade unionism. 'Single union deals' grew in number and prominence, holding out the prospect of a less combative style of management-union relationship, while stemming the haemorrhage in membership and influence. But before we could examine how widespread these arrangements had become we needed an general picture of single and multi-union representation. A redesign of part of the survey questionnaires for the 1990 survey enabled us to draw such a picture for the first time.[5]

We found, in our analysis reported in Chapter 3, that the majority of workplaces with any union membership had members of a single trade union; the proportion in 1990 was 54 per cent of workplaces. However, it was generally smaller workplaces that had membership of a single union and larger ones that had members of two or more unions. Thus the proportion of employees in single union workplaces was smaller than the proportion of workplaces with a single union. The position in 1990 was that just over a third (37 per cent) of employees in workplaces with any union membership were employed at workplaces with a single union present.

Single union representation proved to be a widespread and long-standing phenomenon. Indeed, establishments created in the 1970s, not the 1980s, were the ones most likely to have members of a single union rather than multiple unions. It was only amongst the very youngest workplaces, established at the end of the 1980s, that there were signs of an increasing incidence of single union representation. Generally speaking it was the service sector that dominated the picture; new manufacturing plants, the archetypal home of the 'single union agreement', were rare and they contributed little to the overall incidence of workplaces with a single union.

We found that single union representation was widely spread across industries and involved all the major unions recruiting in industry and commerce. Some industries with a high incidence of single unionism were industries where few workplaces had any union members; in other industries it was the opposite. In some industries a single union accounted for most of the unionised workplaces. In others, several unions were present and appeared to compete. In some of these the big general unions competed with each other; in others they competed with more specialised unions that recruited in a limited range of industries or occupations. While Britain is well known for its complex, multi-union arrangements, even in terms of single union representation the picture derived from our analysis was far from the tidy pattern evident in many other industrialised countries. And the unions most commonly involved were not the ones associated with the new 'single union agreements' of the 1980s.

Compared with multi-union workplaces, our analysis suggested that sites that had a single union present generally had weaker forms of unionism. Membership density averaged 46 per cent of employees in workplaces with a single union compared with 72 per cent in multi-union establishments. Workforce size accounted for little of this difference. Two main factors lay behind the much lower levels of membership in single union workplaces.

First, the types of employee in membership were much more commonly confined to one section of the workforce, usually manual workers. This appeared to reflect the traditional recruitment policies of many of the unions involved – and possibly their difficulty in spreading their appeal to employees in white-collar occupations. There was also evidence of management attitudes unfavourable to trade unions in many single union workplaces.

Secondly, and crucially, recognition by management for collective bargaining was substantially less likely in single union than in multi-union workplaces. Where there was recognition it covered a smaller proportion of the workforce. Thus among workplaces with a single recognised union 66 per cent of employees were covered by collective agreements; the figure was 86 per cent where there were multiple recognised unions. Other indicators of union strength mostly reinforced the conclusion that single union representation was generally a weaker form of representation.

## Single union agreements

Such was the background against which we focused, in Chapter 4, on the single union agreements that were a prominent feature of the 'new industrial relations' that was so much discussed and debated in the 1980s.

The first element of the single union agreements that we identified was that management and the trade union agreed that management would recognise only that particular union. These 'sole union agreements' were found to be common in workplaces with a single recognised union: over two fifths of them had a formal agreement incorporating exclusive recognition.

The sorts of workplace that had them were a far cry from the foreign-owned, new manufacturing plants of the 'new-style agreements'. There was a heavy concentration of sole union agreements in retailing and in the banking and insurance industries; relatively few were in manufacturing and these were thinly spread across the sector. Foreign-owned workplaces were only slightly more likely to have them than UK-owned sites, so overall there were many more UK-owned than foreign-owned sites with sole union agreements. In terms of workplace age, the results were also surprising. Younger workplaces were no more likely to have sole union agreements than older workplaces. And among younger workplaces it was those that had moved from elsewhere, not original new workplaces (whether on 'greenfield' or 'brownfield' sites) that had the higher figures.

Neither were sole union agreements a specialty of the unions, such as the EETPU and the AEU, that spearheaded the 'new-style agreements'. Industry-specific unions and the big general unions had sole recognition agreements in many more workplaces than these two. Furthermore, it was staff associations or 'company unions' that accounted for a large minority of agreements; there were almost no cases where they had sole membership without a sole representation agreement. This provided some support for the suggestion that staff associations are encouraged by management as a defence against the possibility of trade union representation.

Overall, the evidence was not clear-cut on whether workplaces with a sole union agreement had stronger or weaker union organisation at the local level. Some indicators pointed one way, some the other. However, it was plain that the agreements affected a higher proportion of the workforce in terms of collectively determined rates of pay and employment conditions. On the other hand, membership density was not noticeably higher. Thus more of the workforce were 'free riders' in workplaces with sole union agreements than in other workplaces with a single recognised union, a tendency that was more pronounced in younger workplaces. If individual trade unions hoped that sole representation agreements would involve higher membership rates, it appears that such hopes have not generally been realised.

Besides their provision granting sole representation rights, the second feature of the new-style agreements that we included in our analysis was their requirement that collective disputes between management and employees be resolved in the last resort through pendulum arbitration. We found that procedures incorporating this method of ultimate dispute resolution were extremely rare in British industry and commerce. A mere 1 per cent of workplaces with recognised trade unions had pendulum arbitration and in workplaces with a sole union agreement the figure was less than half of 1 per cent. In fact, pendulum arbitration was somewhat more common in multi-union workplaces. It was therefore by no means a distinctive element of 'new style agreements', as much of the literature has portrayed. Nor was it especially a feature of younger workplaces or of the industries, regions and trade unions in which the well-documented 'single-union deals' have occurred. We concluded that pendulum arbitration was a rare practice, probably not increasingly dramatically in its incidence and probably of longer standing than the single-union deals of the mid to late 1980s. As a distinctive development in British industrial relations, pendulum arbitration has yet to reach the point of take off.

The adoption of pendulum arbitration can reasonably be viewed as a concession by management, since it involves giving up the power to impose a settlement on employees. The next feature of the new-style agreements that we examined was clearly a concession by the trade unions, perhaps in some cases the most crucial quid pro quo of the arrangement. This was an explicit undertaking by the trade union that management was free to organise work at the establishment in any way it thought fit. Our survey questions, addressed to our main management respondents, did not ascertain whether there was a formal, written agreement enshrining this principle; but they did determine whether the way management could organise work was limited by formal agreements with trade unions. We took the absence of such agreements, or other union-based opposition, as indicating that management had complete flexibility *vis-à-vis* the union in the way it organised work.

We found that management flexibility, defined in this way, was widespread. Nearly three quarters of workplaces with recognised trade unions were reported to have complete management flexibility. It was hardly something unique to workplaces with 'single-union deals'. In fact, workplaces with sole union agreements were no more and no less likely to have management flexibility. They simply reflected the common reality of the widespread lack of union influence upon issues of work organisation.

Management flexibility, we found, was more widespread in younger workplaces and, not surprisingly, in those with lower levels of union membership. When we looked only at single union workplaces and allowed for these factors it appeared that sole union agreements were associated with less management flexibility, not more as the stereotype of the 'single-union deal' had suggested.

The fourth feature of the 'new-style agreements' that we examined was the inclusion of some sort of forum or 'Company Council' within which employee representatives could be informed and consulted by management. Only 17 per cent of workplaces with a sole union agreement had a functioning committee or forum of this sort. This was little different from single union workplaces without an agreement and from workplaces without any recognised unions. Clearly the presence of such arrangements was not a distinctive feature of workplaces with sole union agreements. When we broadened our analysis to examine other channels of communication, besides committees, workplaces with sole union agreements did stand out as using more methods of communication than single union workplaces without an agreement. But they were little different in this respect from multi-union workplaces.

Finally in our search for evidence of 'new-style agreements', we looked for indicators of single-status employment conditions. Admittedly, our analysis was based upon a small number of conditions of employment and there could be many more that would show differences of treatment between groups of employee. Moreover, our measures were based upon looking at differences between manual and non-manual employees; not all workplaces have this mixture of occupational groups. There may be important differences of treatment within, say, the category of 'non-manual employees' which are at least as significant as the differences between manual and non-manual employees. Thus our rather crude measure of 'single status' is likely to have overstated the true extent to which workplaces had equality of employment conditions. Yet we found that only around one in eight workplaces had 'single status' employment conditions, even on our relatively crude measure (Table 6.1). Workplaces with sole union agreements were no different from the generality of workplaces in this respect.

### The 'package' of features

Enthusiasts for the 'new-style agreements', and those who had documented their birth and growth, were at pains to point out that it was not the presence of any one of their features that made them distinctive, it was the 'package'.[6] To quote Industrial Relations Services:[7]

> No single element in these packages is unique to single union deals; all the elements exist in other more conventional deals. 'Package' is perhaps the key term, since it is the combination of elements and the climate they aim to create, rather than the so-called 'no-strike' provisions, which in practice embody their major significance.

Our analysis has shown that while four of the principal features of the 'new-style agreements' were relatively rare – with the exception of management control over the organisation of work – the combination of the four features mentioned above was even rarer. In fact, we could not find in our main sample a single workplace that had all four of these features: management control over work organisation; single status employment conditions; a consultative forum or committee; and pendulum arbitration.

**Table 6.1   The extent of four features of the 'new style agreements' in 1990**

*Percentages*

| | All trading sector workplaces | Workplaces with any recognised trade unions | Workplaces with a single union agreement |
|---|---|---|---|
| Proportion of workplaces having: | | | |
| No union agreement restricting how work is organised | 90 | 76 | 80 |
| Functioning consultative committee or council | 18 | 21 | 17 |
| Seven employment conditions the same for manual and white-collar employees[1] | 13 | 11 | 11 |
| Binding pendulum arbitration | * | 1 | * |
| All four features | - | - | - |
| Base: establishments in industry and commerce | | | |
| *Unweighted* | *1510* | *903* | *136* |
| *Weighted* | *1452* | *584* | *131* |

1.   Assumes 'single status' is not present when there were fewer than 5 manual or fewer than 5 non-manual employees.

Nor, indeed, was there a single workplace in our specially constructed sample of new workplaces that fitted the specification. Neither workplaces with a sole union agreement nor any other type of unionised workplace had this 'package' of features.

This is not to say that the research that originally highlighted the 'new-style agreements' was mistaken. Undoubtedly such agreements did and do exist. But among the 100,000 or more workplaces with over 25 employees in British industry and commerce, the ten or so identified in the most recent review of single-union agreements[8] as having the four features discussed above would have a small chance of being selected in a statistical survey with a sample of roughly 1500 cases, which is the basis of our estimates. It appears that researchers have been extremely successful in identifying most, if not nearly all, of the workplaces with such agreements, while from our nationally representative sample of workplaces we can be confident that such workplaces form a tiny – an unmeasurably small – part of the whole picture. If agreements of this type have had an impact on British industrial relations it cannot have been by their spreading into more and more workplaces. Quantitatively, the new-style agreements did not form the starting point for a 'new industrial relations' in Britain. In some senses the attention that was given to the new-style agreements distracted attention from the principal change in industrial relations practice that was occurring at the time – the fall in trade union influence and the decline in the extent of collective representation of employees.

## Human resource management practices

If the 'new-style agreements' did not provide a blueprint for a new form of industrial relations in Britain, did an alternative blueprint based upon the precepts of 'human resource management' (HRM) come to be adopted? Here again our evidence, points towards rather modest change and development, rather than a sea change.

We looked for evidence of the existence of employee relations practices that were indicative of HRM. Of course, what constitutes HRM is a issue of much controversy and to some of its proponents the essentials of HRM are matters of strategy, policy or approach, rather than practice. Nevertheless, some of the widely-agreed constituents of HRM are matters of actual practice and amenable to study by survey methods. In Chapter 5 we concentrated on three features of employee relations practice that could reasonably be regarded as indicative of an HRM approach.

First of all, we examined the methods of communication between management and employees used at the workplace. Here, unlike the earlier material on the new-style agreements, we were able to use the results of identical or similar questions in previous surveys in the WIRS series to look for changes through time. In particular we looked for changes in methods of communication and consultation that might indicate that management was making more efforts to secure the greater commitment of employees through greater participation and involvement. We noted a particularly marked increase in the practice of junior managers or supervisors meeting regularly with their workgroups at least once a month, a practice often referred to as 'team briefing'. Such arrangements were reported in 44 per cent of workplaces in industry and commerce in 1990 compared with 30 per cent in 1984. Meetings between senior managers and all sections of the workforce also became a little more common, with nearly 40 per cent of workplaces having them at least once a year. Both types of meeting became more common in larger enterprises, suggesting that corporate personnel staff – those perhaps most conversant with the HRM debate – were responsible. Both of these channels of communication no doubt provided increased opportunities for management to try to secure the active commitment of employees towards managerial goals. We have no direct evidence on whether this was part of their agenda, or of the effectiveness of any such attempts. But clearly there was a substantial increase in the use of these channels of communication. Regular newsletters to employees might also be used for similar purposes; these too became a little more widespread in larger workplaces.

Communication channels that mostly cater for communication from management to employees are, however, not the most promising methods of trying to involve employees in a pro-active way. Here we had evidence on three mechanisms that might be used to consult employees: joint consultative committees, suggestion schemes, and surveys or ballots of employees' views or opinions. On the first of these there was clear evidence of a decline in extent. Fewer than a fifth of workplaces in 1990 had a consultative committee, compared with about a quarter in 1984. On the second mechanism, suggestion schemes, there was no change. There was, however, an increase in the use of surveys or ballots of employees' views. But our analysis indicated that this increase was confined to large, unionised enterprises and that it may have been part of a move to reduce the role of trade unions as intermediaries in communication between employees and management. None of these developments, then, is indicative of a growth in HRM practices that might be used to increase employee commitment.

'Financial participation' schemes such as profit sharing and employee share ownership are also sometimes seen as a method of involving employees. Such schemes undoubtedly became more widespread, particularly among workplaces belonging to large enterprises. However, much of this growth has been attributed to the favourable tax treatment given to particular schemes.[9] Very few managers at workplace level mentioned any of them when asked about recent initiatives to increase employee involvement.[10]

The second area of employee relations practice that had a bearing on HRM was the harmonisation of conditions of employment. We referred earlier to the extent of 'single status' conditions, noting that they were, even on our crudely measured basis, a minority practice. On some aspects we had comparable data from our 1980 survey and this showed us that there had been, in some respects, a marked move towards methods of wage and salary payment that were the preserve of 'staff' in earlier times. In another respect the move towards equality was more a move towards the practices commonly applied to manual workers – weekly or fortnightly payment. These changes were hardly strong indications of managerial moves towards an HRM approach.

Thirdly, and perhaps the most salient aspect of our analysis of employment conditions for HRM, we looked at the practices used by management to check the starting and finishing times of employees. In a quarter of workplaces with both manual and white-collar employees we found that the majority of neither group had their hours of work formally recorded in 1990. In our previous volume we showed that formal recording of hours of work had increased in all the main sectors of the economy for both manual and white-collar employees. Thus the 'high trust' practice associated with HRM had become less common, not more common during the 1980s.

There are other aspects of HRM which we have not explored in this volume but which were analysed using data from the WIRS series in the earlier volume. Many of these relate to the activities of personnel and general managers and have been highlighted elsewhere.[11] Our analysis in Chapter 5 of this volume has, however, looked further into the relationship between HRM practices and trade unionism. This is an aspect of the HRM debate on which the data from the WIRS series has a unique position. It produced, in the words of one reviewer of the earlier volume, 'the most striking findings of WIRS3'.[12] Given the origins of many of the practices and much of the philosophy of HRM in the USA, it had been expected that HRM practices would be much more likely to be found – and found in their most developed form – in non-union workplaces. Indeed, some of the variants of HRM are specifically seen as 'union avoidance' practices; and some of the large companies in the UK most often cited as exemplars of human resource management are, indeed, non-union.

We found that this was not the general pattern. Quite the opposite. Where 'fragments of HRM' were found they were as commonly or more commonly found in workplaces with recognised trade unions, not those without them. Thus the arrangements at workplace level which managements had put in place to consult, communicate with and inform employees were more widespread and highly developed in unionised workplaces than in the non-union sector. 'Briefing groups', the method of communication that showed the fastest increase over the period 1984 to 1990, were much more common in the union sector. They also grew rapidly in the union sector, but hardly at all in the non-union sector. On a wide range of matters that could be expected to be of interest to employees, our results showed that managers in the non-union sector were much less likely to disseminate that information to employees than was the case in the unionised sector. Furthermore, we found no evidence that there was any growth in the amount of information disseminated in the non-union sector, evidence which could have been interpreted as a growth in HRM practices. When we combined our broad indicators of employee involvement or participation, both financial and non-financial, we found that it was unionised workplaces that were most likely to have either or both types.

Lastly, on the question of single status, the slightly greater extent of common conditions and fringe benefits in non-union workplaces was easily discounted by their greater concentration in service industries, where fewer workplaces employ manual workers. So on this criterion, too, there was no support for the notion that HRM practices and non-unionism were associated. Broadly speaking, we could find little evidence that the very substantial growth in non-unionism was accompanied by a growth in HRM or more 'progressive' management practices.

### Younger workplaces as a pointer to the future
In looking at how the overall picture of employee relations practices and arrangements is changing through time, new workplaces are an obvious potential source of change. They possess the possibility of creating new arrangements, unfettered by tradition and previous practice. If such arrangements were distinctive and enduring, the continuing influx of new workplaces would have a cumulative impact on the overall population. New workplaces could provide the bellwether, the 'leading indicators', of industrial relations in industry and commerce as a whole. This possibility motivated the inclusion of more detailed questions in our 1990 survey about the age and origins of workplaces, as well as our supplementary sample of newer workplaces.

Our new questions on the origins of newer workplaces provided two important findings. First of all we found that only a minority – 29 per cent – of newer workplaces were really new; the majority were establishments of the same employer that had moved from elsewhere, generally taking most employees with them and moving only a few miles. Secondly, we found that genuinely new workplaces, whether on 'greenfield' sites or on sites that had previously been used by another employer, were being created at the rate of about 1 per cent of the population per year. On this basis, the scope of the 'birth' of workplaces to have an impact on the overall picture observed seemed relatively small, although cumulatively far from negligible.

In Chapter 2 we described how these new, original workplaces compared with the overall population of workplaces covered by our analysis: those in industry and commerce with 25 or more employees. We found, not surprisingly, that they were smaller and much more likely to be engaged in the provision of services. Although new workplaces employed similar proportions of manual workers, substantially fewer of those manual workers were categorised as skilled. More than twice as many of their employees worked part time and, reflecting this, more of them were female.

More new workplaces were branches of larger companies or enterprises, rather than independent, single-site firms.

As noted earlier, we found that fewer new workplaces had recognised trade unions to represent employees in their dealings with management. Where they did have recognised unions, it seemed largely as a consequence of the same employing organisation already having such arrangements elsewhere and extending them to the new site. However, many fewer of them had a formal written agreement codifying the relationship between management and the trade union or unions. This runs counter to the general trend towards procedural formality that the WIRS series has observed since 1980. It may be relevant to discussions of the proposal to make collective agreements legally enforceable.

Contrary to what many observers might have expected, we found in Chapter 3 that where they had recognised unions, new workplaces in our main sample were no more likely than older workplaces to recognise a single trade union. It was establishments that had recently moved from one location to another, heavily concentrated in white-collar service industries, that showed a strong tendency to single union representation. However, among the original new workplaces picked up by our supplementary sample, those with single union recognition outnumbered those with multiple recognition by around three to one. Any tendency towards single union recognition at workplace level seemed, therefore, to have begun only towards the start of the current decade. Union mergers may have contributed to this, as indeed they have contributed towards the general reduction in multi-unionism.

Such a tendency has added significance because we found that single union representation was in many respects weaker than multi-union representation. It generally covered a smaller proportion of the workforce, involved lower membership levels, was less likely to entail the presence of an on-site elected representative, and so on. To the extent that this is so, the tendency towards single union representation, among the declining proportion of workplaces with recognised unions, was a further omen of declining union influence in British industry and commerce.

When we turned our attention, in Chapter 4, to single union workplaces, our results went against the common belief that sole union agreements were a feature of new workplaces. Original new workplaces (established between 1984 and 1990) were *less* likely than older workplaces (or recent movers) to have formal, sole union agreements. Nor was pendulum arbitration especially a feature of younger workplaces. If these two features of the 'new-style agreements' had been especially common in new workplaces, we would have had some support for the idea that they were becoming increasingly part of the broad picture. But this was not the case.

Another aspect of the management-union relationship in younger workplaces that we discussed in Chapter 4 was the issue of management control over the organisation of work. We found that agreements limiting management's flexibility in the organisation of work were very much a feature of older workplaces. In fact, none of the new workplaces in our survey had such agreements; they did, however, report higher levels of potential opposition to management initiatives from union representatives and union members. These results suggested that union constraints on management freedom become transformed, as establishments grow older, from individualised opposition to collectively recognised constraints embodied in agreements with management. How far this tendency offsets the many portents of increasing union weakness is hard to say.

In Chapter 5 we turned our attention to communication and consultation and to some of the practices associated with 'human resource management' (HRM). We looked for indications that the gap left by the decline in employee representation by trade unions was being filled by other methods by which employees could represent their interests and make their views known collectively to management. If this was happening to a greater extent in new workplaces then we could interpret this as an indication of the direction of development in industry and commerce as a whole. In fact, there were few such indications. New workplaces – those established from 1984 onwards – were no more likely to have a joint committee or council of employee representatives through which management could consult the workforce than was the case in older workplaces. In the minority of new workplaces that had such a body we did not find that the committee or council met more frequently or appeared to be more influential upon management decisions. Moreover, since fewer new workplaces had the alternative channel of consultation that trade unions can provide, we were inclined to conclude that employees in new workplaces were in general less well provided for in this respect than those in older workplaces.

There was, however, one method of communication between management and employees that were more commonly used in new workplaces and was clearly becoming more widespread generally. This was 'briefing groups', which were reported in over a half of new workplaces. There also seemed to be a slight tendency for management in new workplaces to use multiple channels of direct communication with the workforce. But, as many of these channels were in one direction only, it was difficult to see this as a major development in management-employee communication, particularly of the sort that would lead management to take employees' views into account in decision-making.

In short, our more detailed analysis in this report of the different types of change and of the nature of employee relations practices in new workplaces largely reinforces the broad conclusions of our initial volume. On the basis of the patterns and trends that we have identified – and the continuing existence of a wide range of factors supporting or reinforcing those trends – British industry and commerce appear to be moving towards the situation in which non-managerial employees are treated as a 'factor of production'. Britain is approaching the position where few employees have any mechanism through which they can contribute to the operation of their workplace in a broader context than that of their own job. There is no sign that the shrinkage in the extent of trade union representation is being offset by a growth in other methods of representing non-managerial employees' interests or views. There has been no spontaneous emergence of an alternative model of employee representation that could channel and attenuate conflicts between employers and employees. Nor is there much of the legal regulation that is so extensive in other developed economies to provide a basic floor of employment rights and minimum labour standards. The recent growth in inequality in wages and earnings which has been widely observed to be greater in Britain than in almost all other developed economies is being matched by a widening in the inequalities of influence and access to key decisions about work and employment. Many would argue that this is a welcome sign that Britain is moving towards the type of unregulated labour market that economic success requires. Others would see it as a reversion towards the type of economy that gave rise to the birth of trade unionism in the last century.

Hopefully, debates on this central issue and the many other issues regarding how employee relations are organised and conducted in Britain will continue, illuminated by relevant findings from this and our earlier volume and the many other analyses of the Workplace Industrial Relations Surveys that are now being carried out.

### Notes and references

1. John Purcell, 'The end of institutional industrial relations', *Political Quarterly,* vol. 64, no.1, 1993, pp.6-23.

2. Neil Millward, David Smart, Mark Stevens and W.R. Hawes, *Workplace Industrial Relations in Transition: the ED/ESRC/PSI/ACAS Surveys,* Dartmouth Publishing, Aldershot, 1992.

3. A bibliography of publications and working papers based upon the WIRS datasets is available from the ESRC Data Archive at the University of Essex.

4. These results were reported in Millward et al. (1992) op.cit, p.75.

5. The 1990 survey collected details of union representation for the establishment as a whole, whereas the earlier surveys had collected details separately for the manual and non-manual sections of the workforce. See the discussion in Millward et al. (1992), op.cit., pp.5 and 58.

6. See Philip Bassett, *Strike Free,* Macmillan, London, 1986, Chapter 6.

7. Industrial Relations Services (1993), *Employment Trends,* No.528, p.7.

8. In the review of 37 single-union deals conducted by Industrial Relations Services in late 1992, 11 had all four of the following: 'single status', a company council, 'full flexibility', and pendulum arbitration. See Industrial Relations Services (1993), op.cit. p.7.

9. Tom Schuller, 'Financial participation' in John Storey (ed.) *New Perspectives on Human Resource Management,* Routledge, London, 1991.

10. See Millward et al. (1992) p.178, Table 5.10.

11. Keith Sisson, 'In search of HRM', *British Journal of Industrial Relations,* Vol.31, 1993, No.2, pp.201-210.

12. Sisson (1993) op.cit.

# Technical Appendix [1]

This Appendix describes the design and execution of the 1990 survey, with comparisons with previous surveys where appropriate. Fuller technical details of the 1980 and 1984 surveys were included as appendices to our earlier reports.[2] The bulk of the material relates to the main, cross-sectional sample; later sections deal with the panel sample of workplaces interviewed in both 1984 and 1990 and with the supplementary sample of new workplaces.

## The sampling frame and the main 1990 survey sample

The sample design for the 1990 main survey broadly followed that developed for previous surveys. The sampling frame was the Employment Department's 1987 *Census of Employment*; for the 1984 survey it had been the census conducted in 1981 and for the 1980 survey the census conducted in 1977. As in previous surveys, all census units recorded as having 24 or fewer employees were excluded, as were units falling within Agriculture, Forestry and Fishing (Division 0) of the *Standard Industrial Classification* (1980). Otherwise all sectors of civil employment in England, Scotland and Wales were included in the sampling universe – public and private sector, manufacturing and service industries. In 1990, as in previous surveys, larger units (on the basis of number of employees) were oversampled.

A census unit is in most cases a number of employees working at the same address who are paid from the same location by the same employer. The requirement of the survey design was for a sample of establishments, that is of individual places of employment at a single address and covering all the employees of the identified employer at that address. In general there is a sufficient degree of correspondence between census units and establishments for the census to serve as a viable sampling frame for the survey series. However, some census units have been found to refer to more than one establishment and in others to just part of an establishment. In later paragraphs we describe the procedures developed in 1980, and refined in 1984 and 1990, for dealing with these difficulties.

At the time of the design of the 1990 sample, the 1987 *Census of Employment* file contained just over 142,000 units with 25 or more employees, slightly more than the 135,000 in the 1981 census used for the 1984 survey. From this file a stratified random sample totalling 3,572 units was drawn; in 1984 the figure was 3,640 units and in 1980 the figure was 3,994 units. The selected sample was smaller in 1990 for two reasons. Firstly, the number of establishments at which interviews were required was 1,870, as against 2,000 in the first survey. Secondly, as none of the 'reserve pool' of nearly 500 units had been used in 1984 and the 1984 experience gave a good guide to the extent of out-of-scope and non-responding addresses, the size of the reserve pool in 1990 could be reduced. In the event none of the 357 units selected for the 1990 reserve pool was used.

The selection of units from the census file involved an initial division of the file into seven files, each containing units within a size range: 25 to 49 employees, 50 to 99 employees, and so on. Within each file the census units were then re-ordered by: the proportion of male employees, within the proportion of full-time employees, within the Activities of the Standard Industrial Classification (SIC). Differential sampling fractions were applied to the six lower size bands, the seventh (top) band having the same sampling fraction as the sixth band. From the re-ordered lists, samples were selected by marking off at intervals from a randomly selected starting point, the list being treated as circular. The numbers of census units, sampling fractions and subsample sizes are given in Table A.1, with the figures for 1984 and 1980 alongside for comparison.

The range of sampling fractions employed has been progressively increased during the course of the series. Partly this was because the number of large units in the population has declined and we still wanted to have sufficient large establishments in our achieved sample to permit comparisons between establishments of different sizes. It also reflected an increased emphasis on estimates focusing on employees rather than establishments. Analysis of the 1980 results had shown that employee estimates could be improved with little loss of accuracy on establishment estimates if the sample contained more large, and fewer small, units.

Besides the withdrawal of the 10 per cent of addresses for the reserve pool, the sample selected in 1990 was also reduced by a further 209 addresses from SIC Classes 91, 93 and 95. This innovation was made because analysis of the previous surveys had demonstrated that there was less variation within these easily identifiable parts of the public sector on most of the matters of interest in the surveys. It seemed advisable, therefore, to spread the survey resources that could be saved by undersampling these sectors over the remaining sectors of the population. The result of these two types of withdrawal from the selected sample – the reserve pool and the

**Table A.1 Sampling fractions and numbers of census units drawn from the selected main samples, 1980, 1984 and 1990**

| | Number of census units | | | Sampling fractions | | | Sample selected | | |
|---|---|---|---|---|---|---|---|---|---|
| Year of survey | 1980 | 1984 | 1990 | 1980 | 1984 | 1990 | 1980 | 1984 | 1990 |
| Year of census (sampling frame) | 1977 | 1981 | 1987 | 1977 | 1981 | 1987 | 1977 | 1981 | 1987 |
| **Number of employees recorded at census unit:** | | | | | | | | | |
| 25-49 | 66959 | 70000 | 74956 | 79 | 72 | 100 | 849 | 760 | 748 |
| 50-99 | 33881 | 33288 | 35215 | 42.5 | 51 | 56 | 799 | 650 | 623 |
| 100-199 | 18340 | 17625 | 18178 | 26 | 28 | 32 | 700 | 620 | 569 |
| 200-499 | 10649 | 9880 | 9921 | 15 | 16 | 19 | 699 | 600 | 513 |
| 500-999 | 3098 | 2796 | 2693 | 6 | 6 | 6 | 499 | 400 | 450 |
| 1000-1999 | 1332* | 1169 | 960 | 5.5 | 3.3 | 6 | 249 | 360 | 485 |
| 2000+ | 571* | 484 | 360 | 3 | 3.3 | 2 | 199 | 150 | 184 |
| Total | 134825 | 135242 | 142283 | 33.7 | 37 | 40 | 3994 | 3640 | 3572 |

\* estimated subdivision

undersampling of Classes 91, 93 and 95 – was to bring the number of units in the initial sample down to 3,006.

There were several other minor types of withdrawal from the initial sample prior to its issue for fieldwork. Together these accounted for 135 cases. The most numerous were 'aggregate returns'. In these cases our preliminary scanning of the sample suggested that the census data unit was for a group of employees that could not possibly be employed at a single address, but were from several establishments of the same employer. Generally such cases arose in local authority employment and might, for example, include all the teachers in a Local Education Authority district. In each of the 47 such cases the employer was asked in a letter from the Employment Department research team to provide a breakdown by establishment of the employees covered by the sampled census unit. A response was received in 27 cases, while the remaining 20 employers had not replied by the end of July 1990, despite several follow-up letters and telephone calls.[3] Twelve of the 27 employers who responded did provide lists of establishments with numbers of employees so that resampling could be carried out according to the basic design. This generated 12 units which were added to the sample. A further 12 of the employers who responded indicated that they were unwilling or unable to provide the required information. In the remaining three cases it was agreed that the census return referred entirely to peripatetic or part-time employees who could not be allocated for our purposes to individual addresses. These three cases were withdrawn, along with 18 similar cases identified during the scanning of the sample.

Barring the above exceptions, census units consisted of employees of the same employer at a single address. However, the census unit did not necessarily include all employees of that employer at the address. Other census units relating to the same employer at the same address would also have had a chance of selection if they contained 25 or more employees. If they appeared in the sample it was necessary to delete all but one of the census units relating to the *multiply-sampled establishment* and apply an appropriate individual weight to the remaining unit if it led to a successful interview. There were 15 deletions from the sample arising from the identification of such cases.

In 1984, all addresses in the deep coal-mining industry had been withdrawn from the sample prior to fieldwork, owing to the industry-wide dispute current at the time. In 1990 the deep coal-mining industry was again withdrawn from the sample so that the industrial coverage of the three surveys in the series would be identical. A separate survey of the coal-mining industry has since been carried out for the Employment Department using the 1990 WIRS sample and field methodology.

The remaining withdrawals prior to fieldwork were:

- 10 units where the address was too incomplete to pass to interviewers;
- 5 units which duplicated units retained in the sample;
- 6 units classified as extreme geographical outliers;
- 2 units interviewed during the course of pilot work.

Thus the issued sample amounted to 2,871 addresses.

## Questionnaire development and fieldwork

Development work for the 1990 survey began in November 1988 following a conference organised by the ESRC to discuss the uses made of the two earlier surveys and possible changes, if there were a third.[4] Subsequently, users of the 1980 or 1984 data, plus a number of other academics in the fields of industrial relations, industrial sociology and labour economics, were canvassed for their suggestions for the design and content of the proposed third survey.[5] In March 1989 the Steering Committee representing the four sponsoring bodies met to confirm their interest in mounting a third survey and begin discussions of its general design and method of conduct. Detailed consideration of questionnaire items took place in the months leading up to the pilot survey in late September and early October 1989.

### *Pilot work*

The pilot survey was carried out in 54 establishments, 42 of which were selected from the list of addresses where interviews had been carried out in 1984. The remaining 12 were in workplaces less than three years old, identified by interviewers by observation in their locality. The main objectives of the pilot were to test the content and length of the draft questionnaires and the feasibility of interviewing a financial manager (a new type of respondent for the WIRS series). Because there were many suggested new questions for the main management questionnaire, some of the core questions from previous surveys were not repeated in the pilot for some sections of the workforce even though they would be in the main survey; the time saved by doing this was subsequently allowed for in the redesign before the main fieldwork. The pilot survey included 29 interviews with manual and non-manual worker representatives and 15 financial managers; the numbers of these were fewer than desirable, but they were all that were practical within the short period allowed for the pilot survey.

The main outcome of the pilot work was a drastic redesign of the main management questionnaire, principally aimed at reducing the length of the longest interviews. This redesign had two main elements. First, the parallel questioning on union membership and recognition for manual employees and for non-manual employees was combined into a single section, as detailed in Chapter 3 of the earlier volume.[6] Secondly, many of the background and performance questions which had been asked of both the main management respondent and the financial manager respondent in the pilot were retained in the financial manager questionnaire, but asked in the main management interview only if a financial manager interview was not expected. This substantially reduced the length of the main management interviews, but introduced complications for the analysis.[7] A further reduction was achieved by reducing still further the number of questions asked of worker representatives and the main management respondent. The final trimming of the questionnaires excluded new questions which had not worked well or were considered of lesser interest or value.

## *Main survey fieldwork*
The initial approach to employers to gain access for survey interviews was carried out by the research team at the Employment Department, using methods devised at the start of the WIRS series and subsequently refined. An essential preliminary to this was to recognise that different approaches were necessary for different parts of the sample.[8] To begin with a list was compiled of organisations which, from previous experience – or knowledge of how centralised their management structure was – were thought to require a head-office approach. The list included all large central government departments, a few of the large metropolitan local authorities, all police authorities, most state-owned (nationalised) industries – or recently-privatised ones – and a number of large companies in the private sector, notably in financial services and retailing. The sample list produced from the *Census of Employment* was then scanned to extract all addresses where the employer's name corresponded to one of these large employers. These addresses comprised what was called 'Wave 2' of the sample, the remainder – those needing a direct approach to the establishment – being processed initially as 'Wave 1'. In broad terms 'Wave 2' comprised just over a quarter of the main sample and involved head-office approaches to over 100 organisations. These were made by the Employment Department research team and subsequently passed on to SCPR at an appropriate stage.

'Wave 2' access sometimes entailed lengthy negotiations. In a fifth of the organisations contacted subsequent discussions were required at divisional or area levels before approval to approach establishments was given. The target was always to obtain permission for an interview with the prescribed role-holder within the establishment. Failing this, some cases were dealt with by collecting some information at head office and the remainder locally; generally the head-office information was about matters that were factual and uniform across all establishments, but some of these head-office, partial interviews collected information specific to each sampled address. As a last resort, if neither of the previous two approaches could be agreed, a purely head-office (or regional-office) interview was conducted covering all the organisation's establishments in the sample. Naturally this necessitated some questions being not answered, either because the higher-level respondent did not know the answer or because the question was only applicable to an establishment-level respondent. Figures for the location of main management interviews are given in a later section.

The remainder of the sample, 'Wave 1', received a direct approach by letter from the Employment Department on behalf of the four sponsoring organisations. This described the purposes of the survey, set out in detail the procedures for preserving the anonymity of respondents, referred to the published outputs of the earlier surveys and informed the recipient of the forthcoming request for an interview from SCPR.

Interviewing for the main survey was carried out by 147 interviewers, of whom 46 had interviewed before on the WIRS series. Almost all of the 147 attended one of the two-day briefing conferences on the survey, the remaining nine being briefed individually by SCPR research and field staff later in the fieldwork period. The briefing conferences were conducted in January by the SCPR members of the research team in conjunction with those from the Employment Department, the Policy Studies Institute and ACAS. They involved a full description of the survey design, the definition of establishments in doubtful cases, contact procedures, the selection of respondents and a complete dummy run of the questionnaires. Written interviewers' instructions amounted to some 50 pages.

Fieldwork began by interviewers making telephone contact with each sampled establishment, identifying the main management respondent and establishing that he or she had received the initial approach letter from the Employment Department. After giving any further explanations about the nature and purpose of the survey and obtaining the respondent's agreement to be interviewed, the interviewer sent a letter of confirmation – together with a small pre-interview questionnaire about numbers of employees, called the *Basic Workforce Data Sheet (BWDS)*. Over 90 per cent of these were completed before or at the start of the interview, mostly by the respondent or an assistant; the remainder were completed later and returned to SCPR separately. In the latter cases the basic totals had been agreed with the respondent at the start of the interview.

Interviewing started in late January 1990, shortly after the main interviewer briefings, and continued until September, with the bulk of interviews taking place in February to May. The median date for the main management interviews was late March, compared with May in 1984 and June in 1980. For financial managers the median was mid April 1990, with nearly 80 per cent of interviews being held at a later date than the main management interview. For manual worker representatives, the median date was also mid April; for non-manual representatives it was the beginning of May. In both cases just over 80 per cent of interviews were held on a later visit than the main management interview. The timing of interviews largely reflected the release of establishment addresses to interviewers, with 'Wave 2' addresses being later than 'Wave 1'. Large organisations earmarked for initial approaches to head offices thus featured in the later stages of fieldwork, with nationalised industries in particular being towards the tail end.

Interview lengths were similar to those in previous surveys. The main management interview lasted a mean of 99 minutes, with a median length of 93 minutes. The primary determinant of length was the complexity of trade union representation: in establishments with five or more recognised trade unions the mean length of the main management interview was nearly 120 minutes; in unionised establishments as a whole it was 108 minutes; and in establishments with no recognised unions it was 80 minutes. The supplementary interviews were almost always much shorter. Those with financial managers lasted a mean of 36 minutes; those with manual and non-manual worker representatives lasted 45 and 46 minutes on average respectively. The latter average lengths were very similar to those for previous surveys.

As before, fieldwork quality control consisted of two distinct procedures, one applying to every interviewer and the other applying to every completed set of questionnaires. The first of these procedures consisted of a full clerical check on the first questionnaires of each interviewer; any errors or substantial omissions were documented and reported back to the interviewer for amendment, sometimes by further reference to the respondent by telephone. These early work checks covered 240 questionnaire sets, nearly 10 per cent of the achieved sample (both main and panel). The second procedure, the 'structure check', was applied to all completed questionnaire sets sent in by interviewers. It consisted of transcribing a number of the fundamental items of information from the questionnaire on to a form so that the research team could assess the basic internal consistency of the set of interviews and confirm that the correct establishment had been interviewed about. Queries arising from this procedure were resolved by reference back to interviewers or their supervisors.

Further quality control measures involved a postal check on a 20 per cent random sub-sample of establishments after the fieldwork period was over. The letters of thanks and short forms for comments about the interview were sent to 875 respondents at 473 establishments; replies were received from 90 per cent of establishments and 76 per cent of interviewees. Nearly a half of the forms returned were without comment (much the same as in earlier surveys). The majority of comments about the main management questionnaire were critical of its length, its inapplicability to the particular circumstances of the respondent's establishment or the difficulty of some of the questions. Such comments reflected the difficulty of designing a standardised questionnaire for use across a vast range of types of work organisation and were similar to those given on previous surveys.

**Overall response**
The outcome of the sampling, initial approach and fieldwork operations for the 1990 main sample may be judged from the summary statistics in Table A.2, which also contains the equivalent 1980 and 1984 figures. (The 135 addresses withdrawn prior to issue have already been discussed in an earlier section.) Ineligible or out-of-scope addresses, as before, fell into three main groups: those which were found to have closed down between the taking of the census in September 1987 and interviewing in early 1990, of which there were 143; those which were found to have fewer than 25 employees, of which there were 179; and those which were found to be vacant or demolished premises or where the establishment had moved, leaving no trace of its new whereabouts, of which there were 74. In broad proportionate terms these three main groups were similar in size to previous occasions.

Non-productive addresses also fell into three main groups: those for which a refusal was received at the Employment Department in response to the original letter, of which there were only 36 cases; those for which a refusal was received by the SCPR interviewer or at SCPR offices, of which there were 334; and those at which no effective contact was made (40 cases) or at which questionnaires were completed but could not be used (21 cases). These were also very similar to previous occasions except for the number of refusals arising from the initial letter. The very large fall from 220 in 1984 to 36 in 1990 in the number of direct refusals to the Department was partly the result of an alteration to the text of the approach letter. New legislation governing the use of Census of Employment returns for

143

**Table A.2  Summary of fieldwork response for main samples, 1980, 1984 and 1990**

*Numbers*

|  | 1980 | Addresses 1984 | 1990 |
|---|---|---|---|
| Initial sample (less reserve) | 3307 | 3154 | 3006[1] |
| Resampled units[2] | 25 | 55 | 17 |
| Total sample | 3332 | 3209 | 3023 |
| *Less:* | | | |
| Withdrawn at sampling stage | 205 | 135 | 135 |
| Ineligible/out-of-scope | 376 | 449 | 396 |
| Non-productive addresses | 686 | 606 | 431 |
| Interviews achieved | 2040 | 2019 | 2061 |

1    Excludes 210 units deleted to achieve under-sampling of SIC Classes 91, 93 and 95.

2    Units resampled from aggregate census returns, including five generated during fieldwork in 1990.

government sponsored research had made it possible to advise sampled employers directly that they would be contacted by interviewers, rather than request a response to the Employment Department first. Other factors that may have contributed to the reduced number of refusals were: the endorsement of the survey by senior officials of the Confederation of British Industry and the Trades Union Congress; and the reputation of the WIRS series among those with a serious interest in industrial relations research or practice.

The overall response rate, judged by the completion of at least a satisfactory management interview and *Basic Workforce Data Sheet*, was 82.7 per cent. This is some six percentage points higher than that achieved in 1984 and eight points higher than in 1980.

The response rate was analyzed by region, industrial activity and establishment size. In regional terms there was a little more variation than before, with the Midlands being lowest at 77 per cent and Wales, East Anglia and Northern England being highest at 88 per cent. Every one of the 11 regions registered an improvement in the response rate compared with 1984, markedly so in the cases of Wales, Yorkshire and Humberside, and Scotland.

The range of response rates for different industrial sectors was again rather greater than for regions. In 1990 it varied from 73 per cent for Construction to 88 per cent for SIC Division 2 (Extraction; Metal, Mineral and Chemical Manufacture). Six out of the nine SIC Divisions registered an improvement compared to 1984 and there was less variation between industrial sectors than in the earlier surveys.

The pattern of response in relation to size of unit[9] was similar to previous surveys, the response rate generally increasing with size. It ranged from 75 per cent among units with 25 to 49 employees to 87 per cent among units with 1,000 to 1,999 employees. The range of response rates by size was similar to that for 1984, which was a little higher than in 1980.

Our discussion of the response so far has been based upon the achievement of a successful interview with a main management respondent (plus a completed Basic Workforce Data Sheet). As mentioned earlier, not all of these interviews were with a manager who was based at the sampled establishment. In fact, 1,697 (82 per cent) of them were, compared with 90 per cent in 1984. Of the remainder, 134 cases were at the organisation's head office, 136 were at an intermediate regional or divisional office, and 94 were split between two or more sites. Apart from the 94 multi-site interviews, there were two or more respondents for the main management interview in an additional 131 cases.

### Response among worker representatives and financial managers

The selection of additional respondents depended upon circumstances identified during the course of the main management interview, as discussed earlier. Of the 2,061 productive cases, 1,831 employed manual workers and, of these, 1,134 were identified as having recognised unions covering manual workers. However, 205 of these had no union representative on site, leaving 929 cases where an interview with a manual union representative was required. Interviews were obtained in 726 cases, a response rate of 78 per cent, a little lower than in 1984 (79 per cent) and 1980 (84 per cent). Corresponding figures for non-manual representatives are also shown in Table A.3.

As in previous surveys, the major reason for failing to obtain an interview with a worker representative was the refusal to grant permission by management, usually at the workplace. A half of missing interviews were due to this, very similar to the proportions for previous surveys. The next most common reason was that the representative was never available, accounting for just over a fifth of cases. Some of these, perhaps most, could well have been tacit refusals; explicit refusals by the representatives themselves accounted for no more than 4 per cent of missing interviews. In several cases trade union officials contacted the Trades Union Congress or the Employment Department for clarification of the objectives and methods of the survey. There were no recorded cases of refusal by the trade union to which the representative belonged.

**Table A.3   The selection and achivement of interviews with union representatives, 1990**

*Numbers*

|  | Manual | Non-manual |
|---|---|---|
| None of these employees present | 230 | 3 |
| No union members among these employees | 474 | 709 |
| No recognised unions for these members | 121 | 119 |
| No negotiating group consisting of unions predominantly representing these employees | 102 | 158 |
| Appropriate negotiating group, but no representative on site | 205 | 228 |
| Union representative present and: |  |  |
| - interview achieved | 726 | 670 |
| - interview required but not achived | 203 | 174 |
| Total | 2061 | 2061 |

If we take the two categories, 'refusal by representative' and 'never available' as our measure of the unwillingness of union representatives to be interviewed, this element of non-response among manual representatives decreased from 38 per cent in 1984 to 25 per cent in 1990. The decrease among non-manual representatives was similar, from 41 per cent in 1984 to 24 per cent in 1990. It seems possible that trade union opposition to government policy on industrial relations, which contributed to the increase in refusals by union representatives in our 1984 survey compared with 1980, had abated somewhat by 1990.

A further requirement of the 1990 survey design, not featured in either of its predecessors, was an interview with worker representatives in situations where manual/non-manual employees were present but not represented by recognised trade unions. The existence of such representatives was ascertained in the main management interview when respondents were asked if there was a committee of manual/non-manual representatives which discussed with management matters affecting manual/non-manual workers. A further question ascertained if there was a senior worker representative on site. In 41 establishments such a representative was reported in respect of manual workers; in 66 cases there was an equivalent representative for non-manual workers. Interviews were achieved in 63 per cent and 67 per cent of these cases respectively. As with union representatives, refusal by management was the most common reason for an interview not taking place.

The additional interview with a financial manager, another innovation in the 1990 survey, also depended on information gained during the course of the main management interview. As with the 1984 selection of works managers, the requirement for a financial manager interview depended on establishing that the main management interview was with a specialist in industrial, employee or staff relations or in personnel. This was achieved by ascertaining that the words 'personnel', 'human or manpower resources' or 'industrial, employee or staff relations' occurred in the main management respondent's job title and also that they did not have responsibility for financial management at the establishment. Financial manager interviews were required only in industrial and commercial establishments, of which there were 1,510 in the achieved sample. At 667 of them the main management respondent was a personnel specialist in the terms described above, but in 66 of these there was no identifiable financial manager at the establishment. Of the remaining 601 establishments, financial managers were successfully interviewed in 454 cases, a response rate of 76 per cent.

The most common reason for the absence of a financial manager interview was a refusal by the main management respondent to effect an introduction to an appropriate person. There were 101 such cases. However, in 83 of these the main respondent agreed to answer the abbreviated set of equivalent questions in the main management interview schedule (which had been skipped because they were a specialist). The second most common reason for lack of a financial manager interview was refusal by the potential respondent (24 cases). In 18 of these the abbreviated set of equivalent questions was answered by the main management respondent.

### Coding and editing of the data
Coding and editing of the completed questionnaires was carried out between February 1990 and January 1991. It was done by a small team of experienced clerical workers, most of whom had worked on the earlier surveys. There was also substantial involvement by research team members.

Particular attention was paid to the *Basic Workforce Data Sheets*. Obscurities or inconsistencies in their completion were the most common reasons for referring back to interviewers, but only major problems were dealt with in this way. In less substantial cases the research team were able to modify the *BWDS* figures on the basis of information contained in the body of the questionnaires or to rectify inconsistencies. Internal inconsistencies in the 35 numeric fields on the *BWDS* concerning current numbers of employees were noted in 509 of the 2,061 cases in the main sample. In 202 cases the errors were minor, involving a discrepancy of ten per cent or less between subtotals; such discrepancies were left. More sizeable – those involving more than ten per cent of a subtotal or at least 25 employees – were examined by the research team and resolved wherever possible. Altogether 307 such cases were found, and in 302 of these the problems were resolved so that no inconsistencies remained. In 33 cases there were inconsistencies which could not be resolved and these were left unamended. All these cases with initial discrepancies at the coding stage, whether resolved or not, are identified in the dataset with appropriate codes. Analysis of these codes using many characteristics of the establishment and several concerning details of the interview and respondent has failed to show any significant correlations and it appears that the sources of the initial errors are randomly distributed in the sample.

Computer editing of the data was carried out in two stages. The first edit program consisted of a rigorous check of ranges and filters and questionnaire structure. Inspection of the questionnaires and any corrections required at this stage were carried out by the coding team. The second edit program comprised a number of logic checks, checks on extreme values and on relatively complex relationships between different sections of the questionnaires. Inspection of the questionnaires and any corrections to the data at this stage were carried out by the research team. In 21 cases the questionnaire sets were rejected as too incomplete, obscure or internally inconsistent to be usable.

When all of this editing work was complete the achieved sample was compared with the population from which it was drawn (the 1987 *Census of Employment*) and, subsequently, to the 1989 Census results and extrapolations up to March 1990. These comparisons helped determine the final details of the weighting scheme to be used in the analysis. The complete data file incorporating the initial weighting scheme was handed over by SCPR to the Employment Department in February 1991. The final form of the second weighting scheme was held back until the 1989 Census results became available in March 1991 and was incorporated into the final version of the dataset delivered in June 1991. Further detailed work on the file was also done by SCPR in order to provide an anonymised version for the ESRC Data Archive. This was sent to the Archive in September 1991 and made available to researchers from the beginning of February 1992 under conditions specified by the WIRS Steering Committee.

**Weighting of the main sample data**

All of the results presented in the main text of this report and the earlier volume, unless otherwise stated, have been adjusted by weighting factors derived from two separate stages of calculation. The first stage compensated for the inequalities of selection that were introduced by the differential sampling of census units according to their number of employees. This first stage of weighting is imperative, otherwise the results from each size stratum simply cannot be added together to provide a meaningful aggregate. The second, and additional, stage of weighting was applied in order to adjust for the observed under-representation of small establishments in the distribution resulting from the first stage. Details of the two stages are discussed in turn.

Where the sampled census units corresponded precisely to an establishment (83 per cent of cases), the first stage of weighting involved applying a stratum weight corresponding to the inverse of the probability of selection of census units in that size stratum. There were 12 such stratum weights in the 1990 survey; six for SIC Classes 91, 93 and 95, which were undersampled for reasons given earlier; and six for the other SIC Classes. In the remaining cases an individual weight was calculated, reflecting the fact that establishments comprising more than one census unit had greater probabilities of selection. Such cases were identified using the same procedure as that used in 1984. This entailed the Employment Department members of the research team listing all census units in the same postcode as all those in the achieved sample and then combing the lists for any instances of units of the same employer with the same postcode as those in the achieved sample. This procedure revealed 345 such multiple-census-unit establishments among the achieved sample, compared with 300 in 1984.

The second stage of weighting compensates for the fact that the achieved sample includes too few small establishments. This is because establishments which closed down or shrank to less than 25 employees between the Census in September 1987 and fieldwork in early 1990 are not offset by their opposites – those that grew to at least 25 employees, or were set up after September 1987 and employed at least 25 employees, by early 1990. Further details are given in SCPR's Technical Report (Section 8).[10]
The additional factors derived from the second stage of weighting are incorporated into a single set of weights, representing both stages, which are referred to as the second weighting scheme. It is this that we have applied throughout this report and strongly recommend other analysts of the data to use also.

**Table A.4  Comparison, by employment size, of sample after second weighting and estimated population, 1990**

|  | Estimated population | | Survey sample after second weighting | |
|---|---|---|---|---|
|  | Employees (thousands) | Employees per unit | Employees (thousands) | Employees per unit |
| Total | 15303 | 101.3 | 15423 | 102.1 |
| **Size of unit (employees)** | | | | |
| 25-49 | 2725 | 34.0 | 2896 | 36.2 |
| 50-99 | 2605 | 69.0 | 2618 | 69.3 |
| 100-199 | 2624 | 137.3 | 2634 | 137.8 |
| 200-499 | 3065 | 300.1 | 3072 | 300.8 |
| 500-999 | 1770 | 679.7 | 1782 | 684.2 |
| 1000-1999 | 1263 | 1349.4 | 1277 | 1364.3 |
| 2000 or more | 1251 | 3353.9 | 1146 | 3070.7 |

The size match between the sample, applying the second weighting scheme, and the adjusted population is given in Table A.4.

### The 1984-1990 trading sector panel sample

Besides the main cross-sectional survey which has been discussed in this Appendix so far, the 1990 WIRS contained a 'panel' sample consisting of establishments which had been included in the 1984 survey. The idea of including a panel in the design had emerged early in the life of the WIRS series and an experimental panel sample of 235 cases that had been interviewed in 1980 was included in the 1984 survey. In practical fieldwork terms the experiment had raised few difficulties and the analysis contained in our report on the 1984 results gave some indications of how a panel sample could augment or modify interpretations of changes apparent from comparing the 1980 and 1984 cross-sectional samples. However, very few users of the 1984 data made use of the panel sample and this was held to be because of its small size and the computational difficulties of setting it up. The report of some methodological work,[11] commissioned by the Employment Department, recommended an enlarged panel sample in any future surveys in the WIRS series; discussions with experienced analysts of the WIRS data during the development stage of the 1990 survey elicited strong support for this. Because of budget limitations it was subsequently agreed that it should be confined in scope to the industrial and commercial sectors of the economy – the 'trading sector' – with a target sample of between 375 and 400 cases.

The 1984 main sample contained 1,385 trading sector establishments from which to draw the sample for 1990 panel interviews. It was assumed that a considerable proportion of those in the smallest size band (25 to 49 employees) would have closed down in the intervening six years and so all cases in this size band were included. All the largest establishments were also retained because there were relatively few of them to begin with. For the remainder a sampling fraction of six in ten was used. Prior to this, 48 cases where the management respondent in 1984 had not agreed to be re-contacted were withdrawn. A random sample of three in ten cases was then withdrawn to leave 704 cases in the panel sample issued to interviewers.

Interviews were achieved at 541 of the 704 establishments selected. Four cases were subsequently rejected, either because of incompleteness or because there were doubts about the 1990 interviews covering the same establishment as the 1984 interview had covered. The panel dataset thus contains 537 cases.

Ineligible and unproductive panel cases included: two that had been used for pilot work; 87 which had closed down or were untraceable; 54 which refused an interview; 12 where interviewers failed to make contact and a further 12 which were unproductive for some other reason (including the four rejected at the editing stage). The response rate of 87 per cent was much higher than expected and accounts for the achieved sample being considerably larger than planned.

In virtually every respect panel sample cases were treated in the same way as main sample cases. There were three significant exceptions. First, the scope of the panel included cases which by 1990 had fewer than 25 employees; these need to be excluded from some analyses when comparisons are being made between the panel results and change between the 1984 and 1990 main samples. Secondly, interviews with worker representatives were excluded, largely because it would be difficult to ascertain that the bargaining unit used for selecting the worker representative respondent in 1990 was the same unit as the one which had formed the basis for selecting the worker representative in 1984. This consideration did not apply to financial managers, who were being asked questions about the whole establishment or its superordinate enterprise, and interviews with them were included in the 1990 panel fieldwork. The requirement for a financial manager interview (specified as in the main sample) arose in 239 establishments in the panel sample. In 35 of these no suitable respondent could be identified. Interviews were achieved in 157 of the remaining 204, a response rate of 77 per cent.

The third respect in which the panel was treated differently from the main sample was in an extra phase of editing. This entailed matching up the 1984 and 1990 questionnaires and extracting from them a number of critical variables to confirm that it was indeed the same establishment that had been interviewed about on the two occasions. It also involved a number of logic checks between data from the two surveys. This process culminated in the rejection of four cases, mentioned earlier, and the application of seven possible codes indicating important apparent discrepancies between the two surveys. The two most important ones indicate that the establishment appears to have been defined more widely in 1990 than in 1984, or *vice versa*; 28 cases were given one or other of these codes and these cases have been excluded from all the analysis reported in this book.

In contrast to the experimental panel sample in the 1984 survey, the 1990 panel dataset contains no 'chance repeats', that is cases which occurred by chance in both the 1984 and 1990 main samples and which were subsequently identified as being the same establishment. Although such cases no doubt existed, no attempt was made to identify them because to do so had proved expensive on the previous occasion and analysis of the weights in the 1984 panel sample had shown that such cases added little to the effective sample size for statistical purposes. The panel dataset does, however, contain cases that also appear in the 1990 main sample dataset. There are 46 of these.

Weighting for the panel dataset involved two stages. The first compensated for the different probabilities applied in the selection of the sample (and any differences in response rate) so that the profile of productive interviews matched, in terms of size bands, the profile of the 1984 trading sector less those that had subsequently closed down. The second stage involved multiplying these weights by the weights already applicable to each case in the final 1984 weighting scheme. The weights resulting from this process were then scaled to an arbitrary base of 500.

### The 1990 sample of 'new workplaces'
The decision to obtain a separate sample of 'new workplaces' as part of the 1990 WIRS project was an attempt to remedy an acknowledged and inevitable shortcoming of the main sample – its age. The sampling frame used for all three WIRS main samples has been the most recent *Census of Employment*. The delay of over two years between the actual Census date and the availability of the Census data for sampling purposes has meant that

in effect the sampling frame has been limited to establishments in existence some two and a half years before fieldwork and having 25 or more employees both then and at the time of interview. The design has therefore excluded establishments having 25 or more employees at the time of fieldwork *and* having been in existence at the time of the Census, but having fewer than 25 employees at that time. The 'new workplaces' supplementary sample was therefore aimed, through a process of 'screening', to identify a sample of establishments having *fewer* than 25 employees at the time of the September 1987 Census (including establishments that did not exist at that time), but had *more than* 25 employees at the time of fieldwork.

There was considerable uncertainty about the size of this sub-population of workplaces. Some analysis was made of the 1984 WIRS to estimate the rate of creation of new workplaces and of those than might have grown to above the 25 threshold in earlier years. This was hampered by the very limited amount of information available in the 1984 survey on the age of establishments and the complete lack of data on whether establishments had been created on their existing site or had moved from elsewhere. On the basis of what was known a target was set of between 150 and 170 interviews at 'new workplaces'.

Various proposals were made as to the best means of identifying and systematically sampling from this group of establishments. In order that the data collected from 'new workplace' sample should be comparable with those collected in the main WIRS fieldwork, the sampling strategies adopted had to be consistent. In particular it was essential that the scope of the 'new workplaces' sample was as comprehensive in its industrial coverage as the main sample. Because the latter included public sector workplaces this ruled out a number of potential sampling frames restricted to industry and commerce or the private sector. The only viable frame identified as appropriate and readily available was the *Postcode Address Business User File (PAF)*.

*Methodology*
The methodology adopted for identifying new workplaces from the PAF evolved as the project progressed. Initially, six postcode sectors were subjected to detailed scrutiny, aimed at matching all the 1987 Census of Employment Census Data Units in that area to employers' names and addresses in the 1987 PAF files for the same areas. This was sufficiently successful to proceed to the extended use of the most recent PAF files to identify a sample of 'new workplaces'. The procedure that was finally arrived at can be summarised as follows:

(a) A stratified random sample of one in ten of all postcode sectors in Great Britain was taken, which covered both the large and small users file (ie. those that received more than 30 items of mail a day and those receiving less than 30 items a day).

(b) In each of these pre-selected postcode sectors the following four groups of small and large user addresses were identified:

    (i) *Group A:* addresses in postcodes present on the 1990 PAF, but not present in 1987,

    (ii) *Group B:* addresses in postcodes present in the 1987 PAF, but not present on the 1990 one,

    (iii) *Group C87:* 1987 postcodes present on both 1987 and 1990 PAF, but 1987 address only on 1987 file, and

    (iv) *Group C90:* 1990 postcodes present on both 1987 and 1990 PAF, but 1990 address only on 1990 file.

(c) Printed listings of the four groups were then compared with each other and duplicates removed. The residue in groups A and C90 (ie the supposedly new 1990 addresses) were collated and passed to stage (d).

(d) A check with the 1987 Census of Employment was undertaken and duplicates removed. (Clearly any cases that matched with the Census would have been ineligible).

(e) The remaining addresses were then checked with 1987 or earlier local postcode directories for duplicates, which were again removed.

(f) Next, all personal PO Box Numbers were removed from the list.

(g) Finally, all private domestic addresses and farms (Agriculture being outside the scope of WIRS) were removed.

(h) The list was then screened for eligibility.

The large numbers of addresses involved in the above procedures, and the fact that each stage had to be done manually (as no comparable computer files existed), meant that this was a very time-consuming, labour-intensive and repetitive process. It eventually produced the results shown in Table A.5.

In total, 872 postcode sectors were selected, which produced 8,553 addresses. Some 222 of these addresses were discovered to be duplicates of others within the list and were deleted. A further 132 were removed as domestic addresses and 36 as farms. One other address was removed because it had been used in the pilot work for the main fieldwork. The removals resulting from the other stages of the procedure are discussed below.

**Table A.5  Addresses removed from the 'New Workplaces' Supplementary Sample listing prior to contacting**

|  | Number | Percentage |
|---|---|---|
| Addresses sampled from 872 postcode sectors | 8553 | 100 |
| *Less removals:* | | |
| Duplicates within file | 222 | 3 |
| Duplicated between A, B, C87 & C90 groups | 2634 | 31 |
| Duplicates with 1987 Census of Employment | 462 | 5 |
| Duplicates with earlier Postcode Directories | 736 | 9 |
| Personal P.O. Box numbers | 545 | 6 |
| Private domestic addresses | 132 | 2 |
| Farms | 36 | * |
| Used as part of pilot work | 1 | * |
| Total removals | 4768 | 56 |
| Addresses available for contacting & screening | 3785 | 44 |

## Duplicates between A, B, C87 & C90 Groups

2,634 addresses were deleted as being duplicated between these groups. The majority of these were addresses that appeared in both the C90 file and the C87 file, differing only very slightly in name (through typographical error) or with the addition of 'PLC', but otherwise clearly referring to the same employer at the same address. Far fewer duplicates were found between the A and B files.

When the four files were originally received from the PAF distributors it had been assumed that these checks (between C90 and C87, and between A and B) were the only ones necessary, as the A and C90 files were designed to be mutually exclusive. However, as work progressed it became apparent that in a number of cases this was not so, with there being duplicates between *all four* files. As such, further cross-checks had to be instituted on the remaining sectors, as well as back-checks on the sectors already completed.

## Duplicates with 1987 Census of Employment

Printout was supplied by the Employment Department covering all units on the 1987 Census that fell into the 872 postcode sectors. This was then manually checked against the remaining addresses and resulted in the removal of 462 duplicates.

### Duplicates with 1987 or earlier Postcode Directories
This check was instituted after the postcode sectors sampled in one area (Leicester) produced suspiciously large numbers of supposedly new addresses. These were found to include many well-known, long established organisations and establishments. The check was conducted by comparing the sampled addresses with the relevant postcode directories *produced before* the 1987 Census. The high number of duplicates (736) found at this stage seems to indicate that the PAF files are not comprehensively updated in all areas of the country.

### Personal PO Box Numbers
It was originally thought that personal PO Box Numbers should be left in the sample because they could well be the point of contact for a business being run at or from the proprietor's home. However, after much work on them it was decided to remove all 545 addresses containing only personal PO Box Numbers from the sample for the following reasons:

- the vast majority could not be contacted because they had an inadequate address for Directory Enquiries to identify them, were ex- directory, or had no name attached to the Box Number.
- none of the personal PO boxes actually contacted proved to be eligible for the survey as they either consisted of self-employed people with no employees or were very small organisations (clubs, etc);
- others contacted were used by individuals who for private reasons did not wish to be contacted about them, and, in some cases, were actively hostile to having been contacted.

### Outcome of duplicate checks
This meant that a total of 4,768 (55.7 per cent) of the addresses sampled were removed prior to formal screening. 3,832 of the removals were accounted for by the various duplications with the A,B,C87,C90 groups, with the '87 Census and with the postcode directories – amounting to 80 per cent of all removals. This figure strongly suggests that the sampling frame chosen was simply not accurate enough (in terms of dates or addresses) to provide a good means of identifying new workplaces. This was borne out further by the difficulty encountered in contacting the personal PO boxes and the addresses that were to be screened (see below).

**Table A.6  Addresses available for screening for the 'New Workplaces'**
**Supplementary Sample**

|  | Number | Percentage |
|---|---|---|
| Addresses available for screening | 3785 | 100 |
| *Out of scope because:* |  |  |
| Insufficient address/no trace | 1946 | 51 |
| Closed down | 20 | 1 |
| No longer in business | 78 | 2 |
| Premises vacant/derelict | 10 | * |
| Premises demolished | 4 |  |
| Moved | 6 | * |
| Duplicate | 3 | * |
| Total out of scope | 2067 | 55 |
| Addreses eligible for screening | 1718 | 45 |

*Contacting addresses for the 'new workplaces' sample*
As a result of the removals detailed above, 3,785 addresses remained to be contacted for screening. Nearly all of these initial approaches were made by telephone after contacting Directory Enquiries for a telephone number. It was not possible for Directory Enquiries to supply telephone numbers for large numbers of the addresses because the address supplied from the PAF was either insufficient or untraceable. In many cases two or three attempts were made with Directory Enquiries to establish a telephone number. Some time after the contacting procedure had been completed, British Telecom introduced charges for this type of enquiry and so the cost of repeating an operation of this kind for any future sample of 'new workplaces' would be prohibitive.

As the method of establishing contact via Directory Enquiries was less productive than hoped, substantial work was also done by SCPR interviewers to achieve contact with the problem addresses. This included interviewers visiting local areas to search for the employer's premises, but despite this and the work with Directory Enquiries it was still impossible to make contact with, or discover anything about, over 50 per cent of the 3,785 addresses resulting from the initial sifting work.

Table A.6 shows that a further 121 addresses were identified by interviewers as being out of scope. 98 of these had either closed down or were no longer in business, 6 had moved and 14 premises were vacant/derelict/demolished. A further three addresses were found by interviewers to be duplicates.

### 'Wave 2' approaches

Of the addresses available for screening, 23 belonged to organisations which had been approached earlier in during the WIRS fieldwork at head office level for permission to interview at establishments included in the main and panel samples. Recontacting these for possible additional interviews necessitated particularly sensitive handling. Initially the contact and explanation about the 'new workplaces' element of the survey was made by members of the Employment Department research team. An additional complication concerned the problems which could arise if these same organisations had already been contacted by the Employers' Manpower and Skills Practices Survey, a follow-up to the 1990 WIRS. A further 12 addresses belonged to organisations to which a head office approach from the Employment Department was considered necessary and appropriate. In the event, the head office contacts and re-contacts progressed as smoothly as had been the case on the main and panel elements of the survey.

### Screening and interviews

Ultimately 1,718 addresses (20.1 per cent of the original 8,553 addresses sampled) were contacted and screened. As Table A.7 shows, nearly three-quarters (74 per cent) of these were ineligible because they had fewer than 25 employees. (Although the screening procedure did not record the precise number of employees if the establishment was smaller than 25, it was evident that a majority of these cases fell in the 15-24 size band).

A further one fifth (19.3 per cent) were ineligible because although they had 25 or more employees now, they had been in business for longer than three years and had had 25 or more employees at the time of the 1987 Census. (Most of these were businesses that had moved in the last three years to addresses in different postcode sectors, and had therefore not been identified as being duplicates in the earlier checks). Ten other addresses were establishments which had amalgamated with other establishments.

This left 104 addresses that were identified as being eligible to be interviewed. At 84 of these addresses management interviews were carried out. Interviewing took place between October 1990 and June 1991.

At 20 eligible addresses, there was a refusal to be interviewed despite extensive and repeated efforts to persuade them to participate. Four of these

**Table A.7  Addresses screened for the 'New Workplaces' Supplementary Sample**

|  | Number | Percentage |
|---|---|---|
| Addresses eligible for screening | 1718 | 100 |
| *Ineligible for survey* |  |  |
| Fewer than 25 employees at time of contact | 1272 | 74 |
| 25 or more employees now and in 1987 | 332 | 19 |
| Amalgamated with other establishments | 10 | 1 |
| *Eligible* |  |  |
| Interview completed | 84 | 5 |
| Refusal | 20 | 1 |

refusals were to the ED plus a further six excluded for other reasons, after the establishments had been identified as eligible.

The reasons given for refusal primarily concerned the fact that the establishments to be interviewed about were so (relatively) small, and new. The individual identified as the main management respondent was by definition in a key role, but had little or none of the support staff available in a larger workplace. Consequently there was little or no time to spare for interviews. (In one case an interview was repeatedly cancelled and rearranged over a six-month period before being finally cancelled altogether when the manager concerned moved to Australia).

The occurrence of completed interviews with additional respondents is as indicated below.

*Financial managers*
Five interviews were conducted. In a further three cases interviewers tried but did not succeed in obtaining an interview. Apart from three 'ineligible' establishments (where a financial manager was identified in the organization but was not on site) at the remaining 73 establishments no financial manager interview was required, since the main respondents did not identify themselves as specialists in personnel, human or manpower resources or industrial employee or staff relations. In three such cases, the interviewer did in fact obtain an interview with the financial manager, although strictly not required to do so. The resultant questionnaires have been included in the dataset (as in the main and panel samples) bringing the total number of financial managers interviews to eight.

### Worker representatives (manual)

Ten establishments were identified as requiring an interview with the senior representative of a recognised trade union representing manual workers. Interviews were carried out at eight of these. At the remaining two the interviewer was unable to make contact within the fieldwork period.

At five establishments without recognised unions for manual workers, the requirement was established for an interview with the senior representative of manual workers on a formal joint committee with management. Two such interviews were carried out; two potential respondents were never available in allotted time and in the remaining case management refused permission.

### Worker representatives (non-manual)

Ten establishments were identified as requiring an interview with the senior representative of a recognised trade union for non-manual workers. Interviews were carried out at seven of these. One respondent was ill during the relevant fieldwork period; 'other reasons' were given in the remaining cases. At one establishment without a recognised union for non-manual workers there was a requirement for an interview with a committee representative. This potential respondent was never available.

### Characteristics of the 'new workplaces' supplementary sample

The 84 establishments at which interviews were achieved were all 'new workplaces' according to the definition adopted for the 1990 WIRS. They fell into three distinct groups.

- *True* (original) new workplaces that had only operated from their current address; had been at that address for less than three years; and at the time of interview had 25 or more employees ... 45 cases
- *Recent movers that had grown.* These establishments had been at their current address less than three years; had had a different address three years previously; had had fewer than 25 employees three years previously; but at the time of interview had 25 or more employees ... 21 cases
- Workplaces that had *grown in situ.* These establishments had been at their current address three years before fieldwork; at that time they had fewer than 25 employees; but at the time of interview they had 25 or more employees ... 18 cases

The size of 'new workplaces' in the sample was found to be as follows:

| Size of workplace | Number of workplaces |
|---|:---:|
| 25 to 34 employees | 29 |
| 35 to 49 employees | 19 |
| 50 to 99 employees | 4 |
| 100 to 199 employees | 8 |
| 200 to 499 employees | 7 |
| Total | 84 |

Thus 57 per cent of the sample were found to have fewer than 50 employees. As would be expected, there was a higher proportion in this size band than was found in the main WIRS sample (after weighting to restore unequal sampling probabilities). The proportion in the main sample was 47 per cent.

Of the 15 establishments with 100 or more employees, 12 were 'true' new workplaces and three were recent movers.

### Region and industrial activity

An analysis of the 84 cases by region and activity (Divisions of the *Standard Industrial Classification, 1980)* is shown in Table A.8. Also shown is the equivalent profile of establishments in the WIRS 1990 main sample. Separately identified are those establishments in the main sample that were classified as having come into existence *during the last ten years*. (Approximately 30 per cent of the WIRS sample was so classified.)

The comparisons between the 'new workplaces' supplementary sample and workplaces less than ten years old in the main sample give a broad indication that the supplementary sample is a valid sample of 'new workplaces' as defined for the purposes of the survey. However, no proper validation is possible, given the lack of data about the population which the sample was designed to represent. The small size of the sample, and particularly the small size of its three constituent parts, mean that results based upon it alone should be presented and treated with very considerable caution.

### Sampling errors

Sampling errors for the 1990 main cross-sectional sample are generally larger than for a simple random sample of equivalent size. Sampling errors were calculated for a number of variables in the survey and are shown in Table A.9. The table also gives the 'design factor' which is the ratio of the sampling error for the complex design actually used to the sampling error for a simple random sample of equal size. The sampling errors for the 1990 main sample survey are similar to those for previous surveys for the same

**Table A.8  Comparison of the 'New Workplaces' Supplementary Sample with
the 1990 WIRS main sample, by region and activity**

*Percentages*

| | 'New Workplaces' sample | Main sample workplaces less than 10 years old | Main sample all workplaces |
|---|---|---|---|
| **Region** | | | |
| London and South East England | 36 | 38 | 33 |
| Wales and South West England | 10 | 12 | 13 |
| Midlands and East Anglia | 20 | 15 | 18 |
| North and North West England, Yorkshire and Humberside | 30 | 23 | 26 |
| Scotland | 5 | 12 | 10 |
| | | | |
| **Activity (SIC Divisions)** | | | |
| | | | |
| **All manufacturing** | 19 | 27 | 23 |
| Mineral products, chemicals (2) | 2 | 2 | 2 |
| Metal goods (3) | 10 | 13 | 9 |
| Other manufacturing (4) | 7 | 13 | 11 |
| | | | |
| **All services** | 81 | 73 | 77 |
| Energy, Water supply (1) | 2 | 1 | 1 |
| Construction (5) | 1 | 5 | 4 |
| Distribution, Hotels, Catering (6) | 31 | 28 | 20 |
| Transport, Communications (7) | 11 | 7 | 7 |
| Financial and Business services (8) | 14 | 15 | 12 |
| Other services | 21 | 22 | 32 |

variables, and for practical purposes a design factor of 1.25 has again been
assumed throughout this report. No estimates of sampling errors for the
panel or the 'new workplaces' samples have yet been made.

**Table A.9  Sampling errors and design factors for a selection of 1990 survey variables[1]**

|  | Sampling error % | Design factor |
|---|---|---|
| Manual union members present | 1.6 | 1.4 |
| Manual unions recognised | 1.5 | 1.3 |
| All manual employees in closed shop | 0.6 | 1.5 |
| Industrial action by manual employees | 0.5 | 0.9 |
| Non-manual union members present | 1.2 | 1.1 |
| Non-manual unions recognised | 1.2 | 1.1 |
| Industrial action by non-manual employees | 0.9 | 1.4 |
| Formal procedures for disputes over pay and conditions | 1.2 | 1.1 |
| Job evaluation scheme present | 1.2 | 1.2 |
| Proportion of manual employees in establishments recognising manual trade unions | 1.6 | 1.4 |
| Proportion of employees in establishments with job consultative committee | 0.9 | 0.9 |
| Proportion of employees in establishments with formal procedure for discipline and dismissals | 0.7 | 1.5 |

Source:   main management respondents

**Notes and references**

1.  The material on the 1990 survey (main, panel and 'new workplace' samples) contained in this Appendix is largely drawn from the detailed WIRS3 technical reports: C. Airey, N. Tremlett and R. Hamilton (1992), *Workplace Industrial Relations Survey (1990) Technical Report (Main and Panel Samples)*, Social and Community Planning Research, London; C. Airey, N. Tremlett, R. Hamilton and A. Gittings (1994) *The Workplace Industrial Relations Survey 1990: Supplementary Sample of New Workplaces*, Social and Community Planning Research, London. Much of the material here was originally produced as the Technical Appendix in: Neil Millward, David Smart, Mark Stevens and W.R. Hawes, *Workplace Industrial Relations in Transition: the ED/ESRC/PSI/ACAS Surveys*, Dartmouth Publishing, Aldershot, 1992.

2.  For the 1984 survey see N. Millward and M. Stevens (1986) *British Workplace Industrial Relations 1980-1984: The DE/ESRC/PSI/ACAS Surveys*, Gower, Aldershot, pp. 319-333. For the 1980 survey see W.W. Daniel and N. Millward (1983) *Workplace Industrial Relations in Britain: The DE/PSI/SSRC Survey,*

Heinemann Educational Books, London, pp, 321-33. Complete technical reports are available from the ESRC Data Archive at the University of Essex.

3.  The low response to this attempted resampling of aggregate returns, compared with previous surveys, appeared to derive from the local authorities' simultaneous difficulties with the administration of the community charge and of local elections and, in some cases, antipathy towards central government.

4.  A review of analyses carried out by users of the 1980 and 1984 WIRS data, presented at the conference, was subsequently published: Neil Millward (1990), 'Descriptive and analytic uses of the Workplace Industrial Relations Surveys', *ESRC Data Archive Bulletin,* Spring, pp.2-10. Other papers presented to the conference were mostly revised for publication and have been referred to in the relevant substantive chapters of the earlier volume.

5.  Further suggestions were received by the author at the Labor Studies Summer Institute of the National Bureau of Economic Research, Boston, Massachusetts, July 1989 and during the course of the development of the Australian Workplace Industrial Relations Survey in mid 1989.

6.  Millward et al. (1992) op.cit.

7.  The main complication is that a number of variables concerning the economic context of the workplace have to constructed by drawing data from the interview with either the main management respondent or the financial manager respondent. There are also 35 cases where a financial manager interview was not strictly required, but was obtained. These generally contain fuller information than the relevant section of the main management questionnaire and were retained. The analyst therefore has to make a judgment about which response to use in these cases. Our practice has been to take the response of what we judged to be the better informed of the two on the question being considered, generally the financial manager. A second set of complications arose because the change in design was made between the pilot and main stage surveys and so the revised questionnaires were not themselves piloted. In designing the final questionnaires three questions that should have been duplicated across both management questionnaires were omitted from the financial manager questionnaire in error. The three questions concerned the organisation or enterprise's total UK employment, any changes in ownership during the previous three years and the ratio of labour costs to total costs. The first of these was considered the most serious and was partially remedied by imputing data from published directories or from other establishments in the same organisation. Despite this there remains a regrettably high number of missing values for the question.

8.  Some of the material in this section was originally published as a journal article: Neil Millward (1991) 'Sampling establishments for social survey research', *The Statistician,* vol.40, no.2, pp.145-152.

9.  All the analysis of response rates is, of course, in relation to the characteristics of the census units selected, not the establishment actually interviewed about. For region and industry the correspondence between the distribution by census units and by establishments is almost total, but in relation to size the differences are not trivial. The degree of correspondence between census units and establishments was

discussed in an earlier section. Size is also likely to have changed between the census date and the survey interview.

10. C. Airey, N. Tremlett and R. Hamilton (1992), op.cit.

11. D. Lievesley (1988) 'The use of panel studies in the Workplace Industrial Relations Survey programme', Social and Community Planning Research, mimeo.

# Index

accuracy of survey, *see* survey
Advisory Conciliation and Arbitration
   Service (ACAS), viii, ix, 12, 63, 74
age of workplaces, 7, 13, 22, 31, 37,
   39, 49, 57, 70, 112, 119, 130-133
Airey, C., ix-x, 163, 165
Amalgamated Engineering Union
   (AEU), 42, 59, 123 (*see also* single
   union representation)
arbitration, 2, 63-65
   'pendulum', 2, 62-66, 119,
     123-126, 131
   accessible to both parties, 63-65
attendance, monitoring of, 107
Australian Workplace Industrial
   Relations Survey, 164

bargaining, *see* collective bargaining
Basic Workforce Data Sheet (BDWS),
   141, 144, 147-148
Bassett, P., 12-13, 114, 134
BIFU (union), 40, 42, 59, 60 (*see also*
   single union representation)
Blanchflower, D.G., 33
blue-collar, workers, *see* manual
   workers
Brannen, P., viii
briefing groups, 84-89, 103, 114, 132
Buchanan, J., 13
Butchart, R., 33

Callus, R., 13
Casey, B., 116
Census of Employment, 33, 135-8,
   148-149, 152-153, 155-156, 158
Certifications Officer for Trade Unions
   and Employers' Associations, 60
check-off arrangements, 53-54, 60

Clark, J., 13
clocking in, *see* timekeeping,
   monitoring of
closures, 15-19, 118, 120
collective arrangements, 43-46, 51, 59,
   72-73
collective bargaining, 11, 14-15, 19,
   32, 51, 110, 118-119, 123
   non-pay issues in, 30-31, 61
   pay determination and, 110
commitment of employees, *see*
   employee involvement
committees, *see* joint consultative
   committees
communication with workforce, *see*
   managers
'company council', 76, 83, 124
company unions, *see* staff associations
conditions of employment *see* single
   status employment conditions
Confederation of British Industry
   (CBI), 144
consultative committees, *see* joint
   consultative committees
Cully, M., 13

Daniel, W.W., ix, xi, 12-13, 163
deferred profit-sharing schemes, 98,
   101-102
density of union membership, *see* trade
   unions
derecognition of trade unions, *see* trade
   unions
design of survey, *see* survey
disciplinary procedures, 32, 34, 62
disclosure of information, *see*
   management

discretionary share option schemes, *see* share ownership schemes
Disney, R., 33
dispute procedures, 55-75

Economic and Social Research Council (ESRC), viii-x, 12, 139
Data Archive (University of Essex), x, 13, 133, 164
EETPU (union), 40, 42, 59, 76, 123 (*see also* single union representation)
employee involvement, 2-3, 76-104, 127
employee relations, 8, 11-12, 117
employee share ownership, 76, 98
Employers' Manpower and Skills Practices Survey, 158
Employment Department, viii, x, 12, 135, 139-141, 143-145, 148-150, 155, 158
Employment Protection Act (1975), 115
employment rights, 133
ethnic minorities, 23
executive share-option schemes, 98-99
Exstat database, 34

Finance Act (1978), 98
financial information, 140
financial managers, 139, 147, 151, 159
financial participation schemes, 98-104, 128
foreign ownership, 3, 57, 70, 91, 99-101, 108-109, 111, 122-123
foreign-owned workplaces, *see* foreign ownership
free riders, 59, 123
fringe benefits, 105, 110-112, 130

general unions, 40, 42
Gittings, A., 163
GMB (union), 40, 42, 59 (*see also* single union representation)
Gosling, A., 33
Gregg, P., 34
grievance procedures, 14, 31, 62

Gall, G., 54
Guest, D.E., 12-13

harmonisation, *see* single status employment conditions
Hamilton, R., ix-x, 163, 165
Hardman, A., ix
Hawes, W.R., ix, xi, 12, 114, 133, 163
Holl, P., 75
Hornstein, Z., viii-x
hours of work, *see* working time
human resource management (HRM), 3, 11, 13, 76-113, 118, 127-130, 132

individual grievance procedures, 14
industrial democracy, *see* employee involvement
industrial relations managers, *see* personnel managers
industrial sector, 9, 20, 39
industrial tribunals, 14
Industrial Relations Services, 12, 74, 114-115, 134
industry-specific unions, 40, 42, 123
inequalities of influence, 97, 133
inequality in wages, 133
interviews in survey, *see* survey

Japanese model, 2, 12, 104, 108
joint consultative committees, 32, 77-91, 103, 113, 125, 128, 132

legally enforceable collective agreements, 131
legislation
on check-off, 54
on collective agreements, 131
on financial participation schemes, 98
on information for collective bargaining, 97
on trade union membership, 35
on union recognition, 22, 29, 120
Leverhulme Trust, viii, xi, 12
Lievesley, D., 165
Lott, M., ix

MacInnes, J., 114
McCulloch, C., ix
Machin, S., 33, 54
management
   communication with workforce 76,
      84-97, 103, 127, 132
   flexibility, 2, 35, 66-75, 97, 104,
      124-125
   freedom to organise work, 35,
      66-75, 132
   information collection and
      disclosure by, 95-97
   organisation of work practices by,
      2, 35, 66-75, 97, 124-125
   policy on union recognition, 26-30,
      56-57
   'right to manage', 117
manning levels, *see* staffing levels
manual workers, 11, 44-46, 51, 125
   (*see also* single status employment
   conditions)
Manufacturing Science and Finance
   Union (MSF), 40, 42, 59-60 (see
   also single union representation)
manufacturing sector, private, 20-21,
   57, 111-112
membership of trade unions, *see* trade
   unions
Millward, N., ix-x, 12-13, 33, 114-115,
   133-134, 163-164
Milner, S., 74
minimum labour standards, 133
Morehead, A., 13
movers, *see* resited workplaces
multi-establishment organisations, 4,
   22, 24-25, 31, 57, 88
multi-unionism, *see* trade unions

National Bureau of Economic
   Research, 164
negotiating procedures, 63
newer workplaces, 2, 4, 21, 31, 39,
   48-49, 58, 80-83, 112, 118-120,
   130-133
new recognition of trade unions, *see*
   trade unions
newsletters, 76, 84-86, 90, 93-94, 103,
   113, 128

new-style agreements, 2, 12, 55, 76,
   84, 93, 113, 124-125, 131
new technology, xi
NGA (union), 42 (*see also* single
   union representation)
non-manual employees, 11, 44-46, 51,
   101, 125 (see also single-status
   employment conditions)
non-recognition of trade unions, *see*
   trade unions
non-trading public services, 119
non-union representatives, 140,
   145-146, 160
non-unionised workplaces, 15-17,
   21-23, 78-79, 87, 89-93, 104, 112
'no-strike' agreements, *see* arbitration
notice boards, 91-92

older workplaces, 3-4, 19, 27, 39,
   48-49, 58, 70, 80, 90-91, 107-109,
   111, 118, 120, 130-133
Oliver, N., 115
opinion surveys, *see* surveys of
   employees views
Oswald, A.J., 33

Paci, P., 75
panel data, *see* survey
partial recognition of trade unions, *see*
   trade unions
part-time workers, 21, 37, 120
pay, 105-106, 133
   performance related, 98
pensions, 110
performance appraisal,
personnel managers, 56, 129, 147
Policy Studies Institute, viii, ix, 12-13,
   141
Postcode Address Business User File
   (PAF), 153-156
private sector, *see* manufacturing
   sector, private; services sector,
   private
privatisation, 88
profit-sharing, 99-100 (*see also*
   employee share ownership)
progressive management, *see* human
   resource management (HRM)

public sector, 37, 55, 87, 99, 111, 153
Purcell, J., 12, 133

questionnaire design, *see* survey

recognition of trade unions, *see* trade
 unions
recruitment, 61
redeployment of workers, 61
redundancy payments, 61
representatives, *see* non-union
 representatives; trade union
 representatives
resited workplaces, 8-9, 13, 22, 31,
 48-49, 57, 59, 91
respondents to survey, *see* survey
'right to manage', *see* management
Rosenthal, P., 13

sample in survey, *see* survey
sampling errors, *see* survey
SAYE share-option scheme, 98,
 101-102
Schuller, T., 134
Scott, A., ix
services sector, private, 9-10, 20-21,
 37, 57, 88, 92, 111-112
share-ownership schemes, 98, 100
shop stewards, *see* trade union
 representatives
sick pay, 110
single-status employment conditions,
 2, 104-113, 125, 128
 and trade union organisation, 109
single union agreements, *see* sole
 union agreements
single union deals, 2, 35, 41, 72-73,
 103-104, 113, 118-120
single union representation, 2, 11,
 35-54, 55-75, 121-122, 131
Sisson, K., 134
size of workplace, 16, 20, 36-38, 78,
 89, 92-93, 100
Smart, D., ix-x, 12, 114, 133
Social and Community Planning
 Research (SCPR), ix, 140-141, 143,
 148-149

SOGAT (union), 42 (*see also* single
 union representation)
sole union agreements, 42, 55-56, 63,
 70-75, 84, 93, 103, 122-125, 131
 and channels of communication, 97
 and dispute avoidance, 62-66
 and employer characteristics, 97
 and union characteristics, 59-62
staff associations, 59-60, 123
staffing levels, 58, 61
Standard Industrial Classification
 (SIC), 136, 149
Stevens, M., ix-x, 12, 33, 133, 163
stewards, *see* trade union
 representatives
Storey, J., 134
'straight choice' arbitration, *see*
 'pendulum' arbitration
subscriptions to trade unions, *see*
 'check off'
suggestion schemes, 85, 90, 93-94,
 103, 113, 128
supervisors, employee relations with,
 84-86 (*see also* briefing groups)
survey, viii-xi, 1, 4-10, 135-165
 accuracy of, 6, 9
 data coding in, ix, 7, 147
 design of, ix, 5-6, 22-23, 44, 51, 61,
 66-67, 76-77, 91, 95, 98, 105,
 114, 116, 130, 164
 interviews in, ix, 5, 140-143
 'new workplace' sample in, 6-10,
 19-22, 48, 73, 130, 152-153,
 155, 160-162
 panel sample in, ix, 5, 12, 16, 77,
 80, 150-152
 pilot work for, 139-140
 respondents to, xi, 4, 11, 74, 95,
 144-147
 sample in, 5-6, 9, 19, 21, 48,
 136-140
 sampling errors, 161-163
 weighting in, 9, 87, 114-115,
 149-150, 152
surveys of employees' views, 91-94,
 128
'sweetheart deals', *see* single union
 deals

team briefing, 76, 127 (*see also* briefing groups)

Thomson, A.J.W., ix

time-keeping, monitoring of, 107, 128-129

Toshiba, 12

trade union(s),

derecognition of, 24-26, 33, 119

management attitudes to, 35, 37, 46

managers' freedom to organise work and, 2, 66-75

membership of, 11, 19, 31, 32, 35-36, 43-46, 70, 72-73, 123

competition for, 35

density of, 11, 19, 31-32, 36, 43-46, 70, 123

multi-unionism, 35-39, 43-46, 50, 52, 58, 64-67, 103, 131

new recognition of, 27

non-recognition of, 27, 34-35, 43, 47

partial recognition of, 15, 30-33, 46-47, 119

recognition of, 14-17, 22-29, 36-37, 46-51, 131

and single-status employment conditions, 109

Trade Union Reform and Employment Rights Act (1993), 35, 54

trade union officers, 145

trade union representatives, 14, 51-54

trade unionism, 117

Trades Union Congress (TUC), 144-145

Transport and General Workers' Union (TGWU), 40, 42, 59 (*see also* single union representation)

Tremlett, N., ix-x, 163, 165

Trevor, M., 12

unions, *see* trade union(s)

USDAW, 40, 42, 59 (*see also* single union representation)

UCATT, 40, 42 (*see also* single union representation)

USA, 129

Van Reenan, J., 54

videos, 91, 93

Wagstaff, A., 75

Wareing, A., xi

weighting in survey, *see* survey

white-collar workers, *see* non-manual employees

Wilkinson, B., 115

Winfield, G., ix

WIRS datasets, 4, 133, 150 (*see also* Workplace Industrial Relations Surveys)

work organisation, *see* management

worker participation, *see* employee involvement

worker representatives, *see* non-union representatives; trade union representatives

working conditions, 61

working practices, managers' freedom to organise, *see* management

working time (hours of work), 61

workplace consultation, *see* joint consultative committees

Workplace Industrial Relations Surveys (WIRS), viii, ix, 1-10, 12, 15, 33, 36, 76, 113-114, 118, 128-129, 134, 139, 150, 163

Steering Committee, viii-x, 139, 148

Yates, A., 34

younger workplaces, 7-9, 19-24, 27-29, 31, 36-37, 39, 48-49, 52-53, 57-58, 70, 82, 90, 107, 111-112, 130-133